Self-Definition

PHILOSOPHY OF RACE

Series Editor: George Yancy, Duquesne University

Editorial Board: Sybol Anderson, Barbara Applebaum, Alison Bailey, Chike Jeffers, Janine Jones, David Kim, Emily S. Lee, Zeus Leonardo, Falguni A. Sheth, Grant Silva

The Philosophy of Race book series publishes interdisciplinary projects that center upon the concept of race, a concept that continues to have very profound contemporary implications. Philosophers and other scholars, more generally, are strongly encouraged to submit book projects that seriously address race and the process of racialization as a deeply embodied, existential, political, social, and historical phenomenon. The series is open to examine monographs, edited collections, and revised dissertations that critically engage the concept of race from multiple perspectives: sociopolitical, feminist, existential, phenomenological, theological, and historical.

Black Christology and the Quest for Authenticity: A Philosophical Appraisal, by John H. McClendon III
Buddhism and Whiteness, edited by George Yancy and Emily McRae
For Equals Only: Race, Equality, and the Equal Protection Clause, by Tina Fernandes Botts
Politics and Affect in Black Women's Fiction, by Kathy Glass
The Habits of Racism: A Phenomenology of Racism and Racialized Embodiment, by Helen Ngo
Philosophy and the Mixed Race Experience, edited by Tina Fernandes Botts
Self-Definition: A Philosophical Inquiry from the Global South and Global North, by Teodros Kiros

Self-Definition

A Philosophical Inquiry from the Global South and Global North

Teodros Kiros

LEXINGTON BOOKS
Lanham • Boulder • New York • London

Published by Lexington Books
An imprint of The Rowman & Littlefield Publishing Group, Inc.
4501 Forbes Boulevard, Suite 200, Lanham, Maryland 20706
www.rowman.com

6 Tinworth Street, London SE11 5AL, United Kingdom

Copyright © 2020 The Rowman & Littlefield Publishing Group, Inc.

All rights reserved. No part of this book may be reproduced in any form or by any electronic or mechanical means, including information storage and retrieval systems, without written permission from the publisher, except by a reviewer who may quote passages in a review.

British Library Cataloguing in Publication Information Available

Library of Congress Cataloging-in-Publication Data

978-1-7936-0594-8 (cloth)
978-1-7936-0595-5 (electronic)

∞™ The paper used in this publication meets the minimum requirements of American National Standard for Information Sciences—Permanence of Paper for Printed Library Materials, ANSI/NISO Z39.48-1992.

I dedicate this book to Caleb Teodros,
my seven-year-old son.

Contents

Acknowledgments ix
Introduction 1

Part I

1. The Self in Ancient Egypt — 5
2. The Self in Classical Indian Thought — 11
3. Sri-Aurobindo — 17
4. The Self in Chinese Thought — 21
   - A. Confucius — 21
   - B. Lao Tzu — 22
   - C. Chuang Tzu — 23
5. Buddhist Innovations — 29
6. The Self in Greek Thought — 31
   - A. Plato — 31
   - B. Aristotle — 35
7. Race, Sex, and Gender in the Quran — 37
8. The Self in the Enlightenment Thinkers — 39
   - A. Zara Yacob — 39
   - B. Descartes — 40
   - C. Kant — 42
   - D. Hegel — 44
   - E. Kierkegaard — 46

Part II

9	Modernity and the Sexed and Gendered Bodies	51
	A. Heidegger	51
	B. Simone de Beauvoir	54
	C. Foucault	59
	D. Judith Butler	61
10	Revolutionary Theory and Race	65
	A. Frantz Fanon, Amilcar Cabral, and Kwame Nkrumah	65
	B. Lewis Gordon	76
	C. Paget Henry	81
	D. bell hooks	86
11	Self-Definition	91
	A. Self-Construction	94
	B. Imagination	98
	C. Possibilities	99
	D. Norms	101
	E. Values	103
	F. Reason	105
	G. Faith	106

Conclusion: Self-Definition	109
A. The Desiring Subject	109
B. The Moral Subject	110
C. The Actional Subject	112
Bibliography	115
Index	123
About the Author	129

Acknowledgments

This is a labor of many years, during which time many people have lent a hand. In particular, I wish to thank Professor Neil Roberts of Williams College, who was my first generous and brilliant reader whose insights have made the book what it is now.

A special thanks to George Yancy, a brilliant scholar who embraced my work and made it part of his prestigious press.

A special thanks to my extraordinary student and friend Zac Gorra, of Berklee College of Music—a perfectionist, who read and edited the work lovingly.

I would also like to thank Ms. Jana Hodges-Kluck, a model acquisitions editor, who so ably managed the work patiently and tactfully. And my sincerest thanks to Elaine McGarraugh for her professionalism and guidance to make the book an enchanting one.

Great thanks to Skip Gates of Harvard University who continues to support my work in many ways and also to Abby Wolff for extending support to my work at the Hutchins Center.

Finally, great thanks to Joe Coroniti, editor of *FUSION Magazine*, for permitting me to use published material from *FUSION Magazine: Global Art, Words, and Music* (fusionmagazine.org).

Introduction

𝒥n this book I wish to show the historically generated ways in which the human Self has sought and continues to define itself through what I have dubbed "Self-Construction."

In Part I, I will explore the various ways by which humans have sought to define themselves, all the way from Ancient Egypt in 3500 BC, through the histories of India, China, Europe, and the Americas, to the present time. Part I of this book is restricted to the presentation of directly relevant philosophical texts from the Global South and the Global North, without discriminating authors but instead, drawing from the best philosophical minds who meditated deeply about race, sex, and gender.

In Part II, I theorize about the idea of self-definition by modernity's moral and desiring subjects as they too develop ways of life, ethics, and aesthetics of existence as existentially serious humans. Part II consists of my own philosophical ideas about what I call Self-Definition—informed by Part I but going beyond it—in which I modestly offer my insights to the curious reader.

Self-definition, I propose, is a view and a corresponding practice of consciously cultivating a value, a norm, a belief, a style, and a habit of comporting oneself in the external world, and to the various humans within it. It is an attempt to always live in relation to others, cherished by their recognition, and maturing by their sustained love, respect, and understanding. Stated differently, Self-definition is an exercise in self-construction and through it defining yourself as human, by a sex, a gender, a race, and a style of existence.

In this book, my examination is restricted to philosophical texts only. Historical documents are of course very important, and they rightly bring us the relevant empirical data by which we can test the veracity and practicality of the highly specialized philosophical discourses. The sequel to this book, following the example of Foucault before me, will be a historically disciplined examination—all the way from ancient Egypt to the present day—of the ways individuals live their lives as they struggle to live authentically.

Part I

· 1 ·

The Self in Ancient Egypt

For the ancient Egyptians, according to The Book of The Dead,[1] the human self came into being from what they called *Nun*. Nun is like water: fluid, dynamic, and flowing toward infinity. Long before the sky, the earth, the moon, the stars, and every conceivable created being, there was Nun, so argued the Egyptians. The human Self's self-presentation begins here. This is the foundational ontology of Being, as based on the Egyptian self-conception. Note immediately that Nun is race, sex, and gender neutral. It is formless, undefinable, and deathless. It has always been there. It really is, the *Is* itself, the beginning of all beginnings. We know nothing about its own beginning. It is fair to assume that it began itself. It is the beginning, which began itself. It is the Is, whose *Isness* is a question.

Nun, or Being itself, was always there. Nun becomes self-presence, as an exercise in self-definition. Nun is a self-created material from which emerged the first human self in the form of a god, whom the Egyptians named Atum Ra, the Sun God, who was forced to seek companionship so created the god Tefnut (immensity) and the goddess Shu (fertility) who in turn kept creating beings, such as Nut (sky), and Geb (earth), and finally the human order, inhabited by Osiris (fertility), Isis (balance), Nephthys (protection), and Seth (chaos).

Atum Ra is the first existentialist who declared that he was alone and wanted to be with others by being relational. Relationality, as being with others, is his first attribute, his immediate declaration that loneliness—being thrown into the world—terrified him. The god wanted the company of others and so, he created them.

Thus came into being the sky, the earth, and human beings. These creative activities were exercises in self-definition. All the created beings seemed to wear gendered and sexed bodies, from the very beginning, which begs the question of the status of masculinity and femininity.

What was the genealogy of these gendered and sexed subjects? How did they stabilize their gendered and sexed bodies? Why had Atum Ra chosen to emerge in a masculine body? What is the genealogy of this subsequently gendered body? These are hard questions that cannot be answered with absolute certainty or evidence. I can, at best, provide only speculation.

As far as I know, there is no previous discussion of these questions. Foucault, to whom we turn to approach these questions, does not begin with Egypt. The history of his genealogy is that of the "European body." I suggest that we begin with Egypt because that is where the first self fully emerged 2500 years ago. The gaze on ancient Egypt, in stark contrast to the European project, (which Foucault presents with unsurpassed brilliance), dissects the human body itself, in its primordial beginnings, which the leisured Egyptian elite—the priests, the medical doctors, the astronomers, the mathematicians—tirelessly present with a penetrating intelligence. This fascinated the early Socratics, and of course the two giants of thought, Plato and Aristotle. Theophile Obenga has now fully documented this history in his masterful *Ancient Egypt*.

It is natural to believe that Atum Ra is a male, because his original self-presentation is exactly that. He introduces himself as a god, a gendered self-description. He names himself as a masculine subject, as if that is the only possibility. His self-imposed self-definition is that he is a male. Why is that the only appearance he could wear? He could have—if he so chose—told the reader that he is ungendered, or simply, that he is a he, a she, or both. The possibilities are many, and yet he chose to appear in history as a male god. These possibilities are not considered in this ancient text. Instead, we are treated to stabilized binaries, as opposed to situated possibilities of being. It is as if ancient Egypt was already permeated by fixed ontological binaries, and that even a god could only appear within those boundaries in that particular form. Although, he could have created ungendered individuals, since he himself was created by a sex-neutral energy called Nun. I must repeat that Nun itself, the very energy from which Atum Ra emerged, was sex, race, and gender neutral.

This is an important insight taken from Egyptian history that is a central part of my argument, namely that this insight could be rejuvenated to provide an avenue to think through the rigid binaries of modernity and provide an alternative insight, which we moderns can use to our benefit as we develop our sexual and racial identities. I will address this theme in the last chapter of this book, when I present possible portraits of the Self as a desiring and moral subject.

This imperishable entity is itself formless but became a source of a human form by incubating a male god who called himself Atum Ra. Commenting on The Pyramid Texts (1040, 1230, 1466) Theophile Obenga writes, "The Nun is not really definable. It is a state of the world or the matter before everything which constitutes the universe. The Nun is before the Universe, before the Gods, before the sky, before the earth, before death, before the birth of the Pharaoh himself, before the anterior gods who will create the world such as it is now. This primordial Nun can be related to water, but it is more like a fluid ether, and not real water . . . This Nun is uncreated.[2]

He adds brilliantly, "The world as it is now: heavens, earth, stars, planets, vegetation, animals, man, life, death, civilization, is the work of God . . . hence at the beginning of beginnings, there is God. God is before the world. The world is created by God."[3]

Note the foundational differences between these views of beginnings. For the Egyptians, who were the first materialists, Nun, the self-created beginner of all that is, is matter; for the Judeo-Christian world, the beginner is an idea, an abstraction, a form, a concept, who simultaneously creates matter. The Judeo-Christian God creates himself, as well, and in this he is like Nun, but he simultaneously creates matter, and in this he is unlike Nun. Nun is matter itself, which creates itself, whereas God is an idea, who also creates matter, including something like Nun.

We know at this original stage of the emergence of Being that gender and sex are, simply speaking, not stable categories from which one chooses. They are only linguistic signifiers. Atum Ra chose these linguistic signifiers and legitimated the sexed and gendered bodies, but he also made sure that the gods and goddesses were equal. He equipped the sexed bodies and genders, whom he created with bodies, with reason, intelligence, and functions, and made a male god, Tefnut, a symbol of immensity, and Shu, the goddess of the sky, a symbol of fertility. The organizing principle in these relations is equality in potential and vision. This of course, must be remembered with admiration. Atum Ra, although he created separate sexes, left the power of choosing sexual orientation the domain of the gods and goddesses. His power is purely creative, but not legislative. He left the agency to the subjects that he created. "Kheper-i kheper kheperu." Or, "I exist, and in me, possibilities become existent." The verb *kheper* means to become. Thus *becoming* is the distinguishing attribute of the Self. Race, sex, and gender are too static to serve as attributes of the Self. Being and becoming are two separate categories. They can combine in a different form. That form is kheper, to become. Thus, race, sex, and gender are real as *becoming* but not as *being*, since being itself is a becoming.

Atum Ra must have chosen to be a male god in a natural way since he was not born to any culture, seeing as culture was created much later. So, this god must have first created itself out of the first biological structure of the self, determined by Nun. Thus, Nun becomes the original biological determinant of Atum Ra, the first (Egyptian) **transcendentalist**. Nun itself is the material structure of the self, and the self at that stage was determined to define itself as male. This, possibly, is informed by Egyptian medical knowledge that was highly praised and recognized by Anaxagoras and Aristotle, among the Greek thinkers.[4]

There is another possibility, however. If on the other hand, we are dealing with a mythical world view, and there is no hard evidence that Atum Ra chose maleness as the first form of Being, but perhaps chose to be female or gender neutral, then it follows that the original form of Atum Ra, and hence the first self, had a fluid structure. If that is the case, one can just as easily hypothesize that the first self was gender neutral, or that it was not determined in any stable way.

According to Reed, however:

> The notion of gender complexity is deeply rooted in ancient Egyptian culture. In the Egyptian story of the creation of the gods, the first god is male and female, and its name is Atum. Through asexual reproduction, Atum creates two other gods, Shu and Tefnut. These two in turn produce another pair, Geb and Nut. Finally, Geb and Nut, the earth and the sky, combine and produce the two pairs of Isis and Osiris, and Seth and Nephthys. In the stories of these archetypal beings, Isis exemplifies the reproductive female, Osiris the reproductive male, Seth the nonreproductive eunuch, and Nephthys the unmarried virgin (lesbian).

In this view, Atum Ra was both male and female. The Egyptians did not sharply distinguish gender and sex. To them a sexed body does not have a corresponding gender; since sex is determined as a biological fact, gender roles are cultural constructions. Mummies have been carefully studied, and the sex and gender roles of mummies are not sharply distinguished. Certain male mummies were shown to be female gendered, and vice versa.

Sex and gender, then, in ancient Egypt become matters of self-definition. Atum Ra could easily define itself through fluid categories—male, female, both, or neither, depending on what it must have felt. The determining force behind Atum Ra's agency must be feeling, given that there was no master gene that determined Atum Ra's self-definition. At this stage it is reasonable to conclude that Atum Ra's sex and gender is the first exercise of self-definition. This god must have felt that it was both male and female.

Obenga notes that, "In Antiquity, Egypt stood out as the only country to have truly guaranteed women a status equal to that of men. Since the old Kingdom, this has been attested to beyond all reasonable doubt. All specialists of Egyptian law-Revillout and Paturet in the nineteenth century and recently Theodrides, Allam and Pestman-have confirmed that Egyptian women were judicially equal to men and enjoyed an equal footing, as was the case between sons and daughters."[5] Furthermore, Egyptian women, notes Obenga, enjoyed the freedom to choose their spouses. Unlike Roman women, who were subject to tutelage, Egyptian women were not in tutelage to anyone, including parents or spouses. Egyptian women owned property and had careers. Some were lawyers and doctors, such as Lady Peseshet, who was "a doctor and held the title of director of female doctors. She was the first known woman doctor in history."[6]

In antiquity, women were a divine force, as articulated in extracts from the Great Hymn to Isis on a papyrus from Oxyrhynchus, number 1380, 1.214–16, second century BC:

Goddess of numerous games,
Pride of the female sex,
Thou reigneth in the sublime of the infinite.
Thou wanteth women (at the age of procreation) to come and anchor with men.

It is thee the mistress of the earth
Thou maketh the power of women equal to that of men.

NOTES

1. Theophile Obenga, *Ancient Egypt and Black Africa,* (Trenton, NJ: Red Sea Press, 1996). For background reading, please see, e Velde, H. *Seth, God of Confusion: A Study of His Role in Egyptian Mythology and Religion.* Leiden: E.J. Brill, 1967. Especially chapters II and III.
2. Obenga, *Ancient Egypt*, 3.
3. Ibid., 36–37.
4. Ibid., 51–105.
5. Ibid., 144–45.
6. Ibid., 147.

· 2 ·

The Self in Classical Indian Thought

The *Upanishads*, an Indian classic and an integral part of the Vedas, are mediated by a given sage, generously and critically imparting his/her spiritual knowledge to those who want to learn. Students are invited for an engaging conversation with the one who knows, typically a noted sage. The sage lectures, and the admiring students listen, take notes, and ask many questions, which the knowledgeable sage patiently answers, with enviable respect, compassion, and understanding of the status, capacity, and level of knowledge of the students.

Furthermore, the *Upanishads*, guided by the search of Brahman, remind the informed reader of the Egyptian *Nun*, the absolute beginning. There is a major difference between these two beginnings, however. Nun is only the beginning; Brahman is not only the beginning but is permanently present in the body and souls of humans and non-humans. He is present in all that he created—humans, animals, and plants—in every living and non-living being. Brahman is perpetual presence and deathlessness.

In the Brihadaranyaka Upanishad, a curious female student Maitreyi asks, "My Lord, if I could get all the wealth in the World, would it help me to go beyond death?" "Not at all. . . . No one can buy immortality with money" replies the sage, Yajnavalkya.[7]

Thus, a classic philosophical question about what it takes to attain immortality—an idea that first originated in ancient Egypt—is classically and confidently answered. The questioner and the sage embark on the most foundational question about the status of immortality. Thus, in this master text, the Self is wondering if it could outlast death by buying deathlessness, or immortality. A material worry is shattered by a spiritual fortitude, and the Self is categorically told that it cannot buy immortality, but it can attain immortality by dogged spiritual work that stops in death. The task of the Self that wants to attain immortality is a disciplined exercise of protecting the soul from contamination by the body, by means of attachment to material things.

The question is a very human one. There have always been rich men who have sought to buy immortality by sacrificing to the gods. Plato's Republic begins with a wealthy Athenian elder, Cephalous, who, toward the end of his life, tried to bribe the gods with sacrifices. Cephalous is a notorious model of all those who turn toward the Judeo-Christian God at the end of their lives. Some of the richest men of our time build museums, parks, and universities to establish legacies that they think will immortalize them. All these are quests of vanity.

This classic passage addresses these very human concerns. The sage's response however, is a stern spiritual message that the Self is mortal, only the soul, for those who maintain spiritual immortality, is immortal.

Attachment to worldly commodities and the obsessive habits of the body must be combatted if the Self is to attain immorality, by protecting the soul from contact with commodities that might defile it. The struggle against attachment is the quest for immortality. Attachment is to death as purity is to deathlessness.

Furthermore, the sage instructs the student that the self, which is neither male nor female but a manifest being, must also realize the Self through meditation, in order to realize unity with the Self. The Self, says the sage, is a unity, ". . . the Self is realized as the indivisible unity of Life."[8] The Self is a composite, and, like all other composites, can be divided into parts, most particularly the body, which changes forms from youth, to maturity, to death. Its pure soul, on the other hand, partakes in the nature of the soul, which is simplicity and deathlessness. In this sense, the body is composite, whereas its soul is simple. Simplicity, however, can be realized only in death. This unity is sex neutral, indivisible from infinite possibilities, the very possibilities that the Imperishable embodies. All the properties of the Imperishable are also potentially realizable by those whom it has created.

The inquiring mind embodied in Maitreyi does not readily identify itself with this argument. It will take some time for the student to be awakened to the new vision of the self. We surmise the sex of the self only through the designated name, which is that of a female person. That is all we know, and that is all we can know and must know. The inquirer humbly asks if immortality can be bought with money, and learns that it cannot and that immortality must be preceded by the quest of realizing the Self. It is only after the Self is realized that immortality itself is realizable. The two quests meet at the tangent of death. Death is a necessary and sufficient condition for immortality. Simplicity, also, can only be realized in death. Meditation is precisely what the self must engage when it is embodied in a mortal body, when it is a divisible and mortal thing. The composite nature of the body is a distraction. That distraction can be conquered by a steady meditation that prepares the self to learn how to die of itself, and, then resurrect through death and become an indivisible unity.

At this point in the inquiry we do not know anything about either the sex or gender of the self seeking to realize the Self, so as to become immortal. Soon enough the question of the ontology of the Self, which must be realized, becomes the subject of discussion. What is this ungendered and unsexed self, exactly? This leads us to engage in an ontological examination of the nature of the self.

We cannot see it, hear it, smell it, touch it, or eat it, but yet, it is always there. Surely we can see, hear, smell, and touch the bodily part of the self. The Soul of the self cannot be seen, heard, smelled, or touched. The bodily senses are not sufficiently powerful to access the nature of the Soul. The Soul needs its match. The Soul can be seen and heard by the eyes and ears of the Soul, perfect powers that are given to the Soul by the Imperishable.

The Soul is a Form that never perishes. Imperishability is its unique property. In the language of the *Upanishads*, "the sages call it Akshara, the Imperishable. It is neither big nor small, neither long nor short, neither hot or cold, neither bright or dark, neither air or space. It is without attachment, without taste, smell or touch, without eyes, ears, tongue, mouth, breath or mind, without movement, without limitation, without inside or outside. It consumes nothing, and nothing consumes it."[9]

There is no reference to either sex or gender. It is implicit however that the Imperishable is also without sex or gender, since sex and gender are forms of attachment, and the Imperishable is without attachment of any kind. As pure consciousness, the Imperishable is everywhere, in all sexes and genders, without it wearing a singular sex or gender. The Self is a dynamic entity. It perpetually moves within space and time, by being in space and time, self-created conditions for the possibility of its own existence. Time and space are conditions of its very Being.

When the Self, the Imperishable itself, is fully realized, all forms of attachment are shed. The Imperishable inhabits all forms of life and styles of existence, without discrimination. All selves freely define themselves as possibilities, as freedom, unburdened by situated styles of existence. Life itself is now a style of existence guided by self-imposed and self-cultivated ways of being human. The imperishable is now present in all self-definitions. Life itself becomes a quest for self-definition that ceases only in death.

"The Imperishable is embodied in the unsexed, ungendered, and deracialized Brahman. Brahman itself dwells in the Heart, and the Heart is life, light, truth, space, the seat of all desires, odors and tastes."[10]

Brahman is also beyond death. It is deathless but inhabits selves who are subject to death, bodies anchored in death. When selves merge with Brahman, however, they too attain deathlessness. The bodies dissolve in an immortal soul. The heart is both a physical organ that pumps blood and the seat of the emotions, a life giver; it is also a transcendental organ, which emits truth and radiates wisdom in the form of light, and sheds light on the dark regions of human paths. It clears the way, paves paths, uncovers hidden spaces, and subjects all human projects to time and impermanence.

All selves inhabited by Brahman, who itself in ungendered and unsexed, participate in Brahman's Form, which is formlessness, absent sex and gender. Maleness and femaleness are simply expressions of the self as created by Brahman. Of course, they have an anatomy and a biology, which does not define their destinies, but is a description of the structure of the self. What humans do with this structure belongs to the realm of enlightened and conscious choices of sexual orientation and gendered styles of existence. They are fluid and evolve in time and space.

In these intricate ways, the *Upanishads* gives us a rich tapestry of human possibilities relevant to our lives, as we in the 21st century struggle with sex and gender troubles.

The Indian Epic, *The Bhagavad Gita*, also addresses the ontology of the Self in a language similar to that of the *Upanishads*. It closely dovetails the *Upanishads*. In the *Gita*, the Self is also unracialized, unsexed, and ungendered. The Imperishable of the *Upanishads* is also the Imperishable of the *Gita*. They are one and the same, and the counsels of the Imperishable are delivered to Arjuna, a reluctant warrior, through Krishna, the mouthpiece of the Imperishable. The mystical language of the Imperishable is delivered to a human, Arjuna who is agonizing about choices that he must make in human terms, in an accessible and compelling argumentation of spiritual reasoning. Arjuna listens with an exemplary patience, and Krishna, characteristic of the Imperishable, speaks with authority, insight, wisdom, and love, as perfections of the ultimate type. After all, according to Krishna, the self is composed of a composite body and a simple soul. Whereas the body is subject to death, the soul is not. Composites are destructible whereas simples are not. That is why the Soul, which is simple, does not die, whereas the body, a composite, dies. Therefore, when a person is killed, it is only the body that dies, whereas the soul survives the death of the body. This argument is that of the *Upanishads,* the language of spiritualized philosophy. These arguments are reinforced in the *Gita*.

Krishna repeatedly reminds Arjuna that he should never be afraid of killing his enemies. If and when he kills them, he should be aware that he is only killing their bodies—since they are composites—and not their souls. Furthermore, he himself, should not be afraid of death, because upon death, it is only his body that will die, whereas, his soul, if he keeps it free from attachments to contaminants of the body, will not die.

Krishna said, "The unreal has no being; there is no non-being of The Real . . . Know that to be Indestructible, by whom all is pervaded. None can cause the destruction of That, the Imperishable."[11]

Self's are inhabited by the Imperishable itself, and to that extent they are protected by the Imperishable, in so far as they are deathless souls. The Imperishable, their creator, is deathless, as are the souls of the humans whom it inhabits. To think that the souls of the selves as inhabited by the Imperishable are subject to death is to think that the Imperishable itself is subject to death. According to Krishna, this is a false knowledge that must be corrected, and that is what is being done with Arjuna who represents this mistaken understanding of the nature of the Imperishable and those whom it has created.

The Imperishable can be accessed only through a sustained practice of yoga, an exercise in the subduing of the senses and the venues of attachment to unnecessary desires, which obstruct the path of the self toward the Imperishable. The self, in the form of Atman, must join the true Self, the Imperishable, to realize the Self.

NOTES

7. Forrest E. Baird and Heimbeck, *Asian Philosophy* (New York: Routledge, 2006), 9.
8. Baird and Heimbeck, *Asian Philosophy*, 11.
9. Ibid., 12.
10. Ibid., 19.
11. Ibid., 158

• 3 •

Sri Aurobindo

Aurobindo's originality lies in his extraordinary synthesis of the strengths of the West and the East. He takes the best of these traditions and creates a powerful hybrid aimed at perfecting the self, with the guidance of the Imperishable for the East, and God for the west. For Aurobindo there is an internally generated family resemblance between the Imperishable and God. Both are transcendent, symbols of absolute perfection, and road maps of salvation and redemption for the human self.

Aurobindo's search is motivated by the perfection of the body, so it can be the superstructure for the Soul. According to Aurobindo, the perfection of the body is the aim of all culture. Central to that aim is the use of the bodily senses—pushing them to maximize their power and the ultimate greatness of which they are capable through the guidance of the Imperishable. If and when the body is perfected, its capacity will be maximally perfected. The divinization of the body is the ultimate aim of physical culture as it strives to house the descent of consciousness—light and being from the sky and heaven moving toward the earth—and inhabit the imperfect but perfectible human body. The divinization of the body is the way by which the spiritual potential of the physical body can be enhanced. When the body is suitably divinized it can willingly and ably house the Imperishable in the form of Brahman, which will come from high on and inhabit human bodies.

Aurobindo disagreed with the sages of the Upanishads who insisted that the body was an obstacle for the self, in its quest of Self-realization, and that its senses must be controlled. Aurobindo wrote, "In the past, the body has been regarded by spiritual seekers rather as an obstacle, as something to be overcome and discarded, than as an instrument of spiritual perfection and a field of the spiritual change."[12]

In direct contrast, Aurobindo contends that the body is an indispensable passage toward the Imperishable. The body is in fact that which makes spiritual transformation a possibility. The unracialized, unsexed, and ungendered human body is capable of maximal greatness, provided that its life energy is fully tapped and its potential is maximized by stimulating its "constituent cells and tissues and their secret workings."[13] The body is capable of perfection, and it is only after this perfection is realized that the body becomes one with Brahman and spiritual transformation becomes lived life.

The perfection of the body, contrary to the teaching of the sages of the *Upanishads*, does not require the neglect of the body, but rather its total engagement. Toward this end, in physical culture, Aurobindo demands that exercise and sports must be adopted as a daily regimen of the self, seeking Self-realization. Bodily endurance, fitness, and feats of prowess are integral parts of the perfection of the body. In the first stage, the body must become physically transformed through disciplined and regular exercise. The second stage invites the mind to insinuate itself with the physical body and strengthen it intellectually and spiritually.

The key to the mystery of our existence is the evolution of the body, and the possibility of immortality. Aurobindo wrote, "Health and strength are the first conditions for the natural perfection of the body, not only muscular strength and the solid strength of the limbs and physical stamina, but the finer, alert, and plastic and adoptable force . . . there is also the strength that the mind and the will . . . can impart to the body.[14]

The strength of the body is guided by the power of the mind and the power of the mind is strengthened by the condition of the body. The body needs to be perfectly conditioned to house the Imperishable/Brahman. No matter how perfect the mental state is, the readiness of the body is a necessary and sufficient condition for the perfection of the mind.

The body's readiness is its divination. When the body experiences a touch of the Supermind, it takes on the life of the Supermind; and the blend of the divinized body and the Supermind is complete perfection of the unracialized, unsexed, and ungendered body. This possibility is the total blend of Atman and Brahman, here on Earth.

Aurobindo presents the goal of physical and immaterial culture to be the self-construction of values that provides a vision of perfection as a possibility, to humans. Nowhere in the text are men or women singled out as purveyors of perfection. Perfection as the goal is open to all, men, women, transgender, and others, insofar as they are the children of Brahman, for whom the very idea of perfection is masterfully theorized.

NOTES

12. Baird and Heimbeck, *Asian Philosophy*, 250
13. Ibid., 252.
14. Ibid., 253.

· 4 ·

The Self in Chinese Thought

A. CONFUCIUS

The Confucian self is fundamentally sexed. Confucius picks up the *gentleman* as the focus of his moral and political project. The project of moral perfection aims at the cultivation of the gentleman. From the very beginning the aim of the project is sexist. As Confucius puts it, "The Gentleman follows the Way of self-cultivation of virtue, observance of the rites, devotion to Learning, and Public Service."[15]

Clearly, women are already excluded. They are present only as appendages to the perfection of the gentleman. They are there to help the male subject realize his possibilities. Women are not frequent references in the *Analects*. When they are mentioned, it is only in the context of what they can do for the male and political male subject. Of course, the gentleman's duty includes respecting his wife, so that he can have a peaceful domestic environment in which he can flourish. His perfection requires that he receive advice from his wife. Peace, stability, and prosperity must first be fully present at home, in order for the gentleman to embark on the demanding task of becoming a ruler, an emperor, a noted bureaucrat, and much else. That is why he must satisfy the demands of his wife and his children at home as he begins to work on himself. The stability of the house is a necessary condition for the gentleman's rise to power in the public sphere, where he has to combat other gentlemen. Naturally, the wife is also cultivated to submit to her husband's project and to suppress or forego her own inner desires, and to present a happy exterior. Nobody knows her inner life. It is not clear that the public even recognizes that she has an inner life.

The Confucian world is a sexed and gendered world. Women have no possibility of realization. Women are necessary conditions for the cultivation of their husbands and lovers. They are not expected to define themselves. They are already defined. Their life-goal is chosen for them, by Confucius. They are expected to live out somebody else's dreams. They are taken care of as delicate beings who are barred from choosing for themselves. They are pampered as housewives.

Confucius is the philosopher of Chinese Imperialism who is grooming men to become conquerors, to rule the world with might and all the polishes of gentlemen. He is not interested in legislating a combination of moral imperatives and political necessities for the world. As a nationalist, he uncritically embraces the world of men, and their sexual orientation, and imposes sexual roles on women, which they might not necessarily choose. For Confucius, political necessities govern sexual orientations. Sexual orientations do not govern political necessities. Race, sex, and gender are subordinate to the founding and sustenance of the Chinese Empire.

B. LAO TZU

Lao Tzu's world is slightly more open than that of Confucius, but not so open that it develops new possibilities for women. Women, however, are at least mentioned as soulful and capable of self-cultivation. They are portrayed as beings who can transcend their conditions, when necessary, and they have the capacity to do so.

Lao Tzu is concerned with human nature in total. His project is in contrast to that of Confucius the imperialist, who is grooming gentlemen to rule the world. Lao Tzu is a universalist who seeks to understand our nature, of which women are an integral part. Women are included in his project not as appendages to men but as complete beings in their own right. Women, like men, are Transcendent Beings.

Human nature is not racialized, but it is sometimes gendered, in this philosopher. For Lao Tzu, all beings have an inborn nature. The challenge is to understand that inborn nature, its ontology. Being, for Lao Tzu, is this inbornness. He seeks to dissect its inborn ontology. Nature, according to Lao Tzu, means what is meant by nature, and nature itself is inbornness. Nature is expressed through its desire, such as the desire for food and sex.

He writes, "We look at it and do not see it. Its name is The Invisible . . . it reverts to nothingness. This is called shape without shape. Form without objects. It is Vague and Elusive. This is called the bond of Tao."[16]

Tao is exactly like *Nun*, and Brahmin of the *Upanishads* and *Gita*. Tao is nothingness itself. Tao is Nun itself. It is something by virtue of this nothingness. The Isness of Tao, is its nothingness. Sometimes however, *Tao* is gendered, as in the following paragraph. "Being impartial, he is kingly (universal. Being kingly, he is one in nature)."[17] At the same time, he also says, "It may be considered the mother of the universe. I do not know its name; I call it Tao."[18]

Lao Tzu contradicts himself in a single page, seeking to characterize the nature of Tao. In one instance, it is a "he," in another instance it is simply a nameless, sexless, and genderless nothingness. The contradictions might simply be the external contradictions of the culture in which he was born, or he may simply be internally prejudice, or rather, he believes that Being itself is a male. This vague and elusive nature of Being itself allowed Lao Tzu to define Being equally vaguely and elusively. He took advantage of the nature of Tao as he characterized it. It is simultaneously like the Egyptian Nun and the Confucian male. Lao Tzu is indebted to Confucius and at the same time desperately trying to think outside the box.

One solid conclusion that can be drawn from Lao Tzu's insight is that Tao is nothing, as are the vague and elusive appearances it wears—that it is male, female, perhaps both, or something else: a nothing.

C. CHUANG TZU

The nature of the self is the centerpiece of Chuang Tzu's ontology. For him, the self is inherently undetermined in that it has no absolute attributes. Like dreams, the self might also be a dream. The following passage sets the stage for defining the Self.

"While we dream, we do not know that we are dreaming, and in the middle of a dream interpret a dream within it; not until we wake do we know that we were dreaming. Only at the ultimate awakening shall we know that this is also the ultimate dream."[19]

Again, he writes, "Last night Chuang Chou dreamed he was a butterfly, spirits soaring he was a butterfly, and did not know about Chou with all his wits about him. He does not know whether he is Chou who dreams he is a butterfly or a butterfly who dreams he is Chou and the butterfly there was necessarily a dividing; just this is what is meant by the transformation of things."[20]

The first paragraph identifies several levels of dreaming, which I call the ordinary, the extraordinary dreams, and extraordinary wakefulness. The first form of dream is ordinary. We call something that we imagine and that we forget when we wake up, ordinary, as is the state of wakefulness that corresponds to it. The second stage has another dream within the ordinary dream, just like the extraordinary wakefulness that corresponds to it. This dream is as extraordinary as the state of wakefulness that identifies it as an extraordinary dream. In the end, both forms of dreams can be understood only when we experience the ultimate state of wakefulness. It is only when we enter that ultimate space that we can distinguish states of dreaming and states of wakefulness.

The second paragraph equally merits a close reading on the status of the Self and the various appearances it wears and how "real" they appear to us. On close scrutiny, nothing is real or unreal, but a blend of both. What is even more, we must first ask ourselves, what we mean by "the real."

For Chuang, what we call the real is in fact a constellation of loose absolutes, such as this is hot and that is cold, this is short and that is tall, and yet there are no such absolutes. These are linguistic designations of experiences, which come to us via the senses, as if they are naturally so. They are not naturally so, but only names that we have rigidly attached to describe our experiences. They are, as Kant contends in his discussion of judgements and categories of understanding, conditions that make it possible for us to coherently designate our experiences in a sensible way, and within time.[21]

These are unjustified absolutes, which we have uncritically inherited from tradition. The conception of the Self belongs to this realm of the real, which must be exploded by the forceless interrogation of reason.

When we penetrate the interiors of the real, we learn that the racialization, sexualization, and genderization of the Self shout out for guidance from critical philosophical reasoning. Chuang Tzu successfully provides a coherent, sound, clear, and plausible analysis of the conditions that produce the binaries of language. In this venture he plumbs the depths beyond Confucius, the apologist of tradition, and Lao Tzu, who did not dig deep enough.

For Chuang Tzu, the real has been absolutized as the absence of dreams. Yet, the real may be just another dream. Our imaginations have limitless possibilities. Our sexualized and gendered bodies are merely fragile foundations in which the self is anchored, often by the weight of habits of the heart, and not necessarily as an active self-construction of values. Race, sex, and gender are merely unplumbed self-definitions. Of course, we do not choose to be born to any biology. We are born with certain structures. Structures are frames of the self. There is nothing absolute about them. Similarly, their functions are merely impositions mediated by linguistic designations. Gender is thus a function of sexual structures. We can redesignate what males do as feminine and what females do as masculine, by reordering. My maleness is not an absolute real, nor is my femaleness, nor is any other gradation within these binaries. The binaries themselves are not more real than further definitions for the Self. The boundaries are open horizons and regions of experience.

Absolutes are dreams, as we learned from Chuang Tzu. If one says he is a male, and another a female, and yet another says neither or both, in Chuang Tzu's reading, all of them could be right. That is because no single definition is absolute; they are merely attempts at self-definition. They are, in the end, expressions of how selves feel, and nothing more.

As Chuang Tzu puts it, "My life flows between confines, but knowledge has no confines. If we use the confined to follow after the unconfined, there is danger that the flow will cease; and when it ceases, to exercise knowledge is pure danger."[22]

The point is simply this: The confines that we put upon the self by giving it absolute identities, such as race, sex, and gender, impose boundaries in the form of binaries, which arrest the flow of human possibilities. One does not choose to be born to a race, a sex, or a gender; one simply finds oneself within these linguistic confines of the established reality, called the real. Once we name something as an absolute we risk the possibility of clogging the flow of the conditions of the not-yet, of all that could be, of the flow of knowledge and the construction of values, which could enable the Self to know itself, to define its possibilities.

One is identified by the established reality, and this identity is not self-chosen. It is a linguistic imposition, which confines the possible to the real and the real becomes an absolute expression of power. This kind of knowledge loses its purity. Our five senses impose limitations on the Self. The Self sees, hears, and touches selectively. We do not see, hear, or touch the whole, but always parts of the whole, and that partial engagement is a limitation of knowledge. The Self does not know what it should see, hear, and touch. These objects are not always good for the Self, and yet the Self cannot help but see, hear, and touch what is not objectively good for it. Ambition and danger always accompany the Self when it hears, touches, and sees.[23] These selective outcomes are byproducts of linguistic confines and the impurification of knowledge.

Chuang Tzu writes, "Besides, do you after all understand that the thing by which the Power in us is dissipated is the very thing by which knowledge is brought forth? The power is dissipated by making a name, knowledge comes forth from competition. To make a name is to clash with others, knowledge is a tool of competition. Both of them are sinister tools, of no use in perfecting conduct."[24]

Contrary to the Enlightenment view of the power of knowledge as the dispenser of clarity and precision, for Chuang Tzu, knowledge in concert with language affects conduct negatively. The act of naming puts selves at war with one another by asserting that one name is superior to another name. Names, as sources of multiple identities, put humans against one another. Tension gives way to peace, but sometimes war is the outcome of this unhealthy competition.

In Chuang Tzu's view, it is knowledge that makes life short, nasty, and brutish, as Thomas Hobbes noted in the seventeenth century. The root of that pessimistic view of humans was foreshadowed by Chuang Tzu centuries earlier, as noted above.

Knowledge then does not give us a peaceful character but rather a cancerous one. Knowledge, which is imposed by tradition and is not mediated by deep thought, does not ready the Self for the good life. This kind of knowledge does more harm than good for emerging character. Character is cultivated by a conscious practice of self-improvement as opposed to a blind application of knowledge. It is in this spirit that Chuang Tzu is being critical of knowledge.

Chuang Tzu distinguishes knowledge from spiritual thought. The first is guided by arrogance. The second is humbled by awareness of the limitations of human intelligence. The first is premised on the belief that the self is independent. The second is premised with the awareness that the Self, given its flaws and limitations, is dependent on a power outside of itself, for which it searches. For Chuang Tzu, this is the Way. The joy of the first is self-reliance. The joy of the second is dependence on a superior intelligence.

The undefined Self is a moral project that begins with the self-imposed task of self-characterization. Like the Egyptians, for Chuang Tzu, the self is not a static being, but a becoming of possibilities (kheper), the utmost source of self-definition.

Following Chuang Tzu, we can characterize the Self in the following way: The Self is a composite. Like all composites, it is divisible and is subject to age and death. Unlike the Soul, which is simple and indivisible, trapped in the body, as we learned from the Egyptian priests, the body is ever changing, as it steadily moves toward death. According to Chuang Tzu, however, death and life are not divisible absolutes. They are part of the Way. Moreover, death and life are not distinguishable. We have no way of knowing whether we are awake or dead, we only think that we know these states of mind with absolute precision. Rather, all that we have are practical assumptions.

On these premises, the Self is unknowable. Sex, gender, and race are part of this dynamic continuum, this indestructible energy. When we characterize the Self this way, we are immediately struck by the unknowability of the Self's anatomy. All that we have are ever-changing appearances. It is these appearances that move toward death. Movement, as within time and space, are their inherent properties. While moving, they also change their forms. They are at first young and sprightly, and then wrinkled, frail, and old. These are the inherent forms of appearances. All composites have this essential nature, totally unlike the nature of simples, whose essential property is deathlessness, permanence, and movement in the form of ceaseless becoming. In these readings, sex, race, and gender also have the appearance of ceaseless movement and perpetual self-invention, which cease with the death of the body—the bearer of race, sex, and gender.

The following passage makes this point, "What is It is also Other, what is Other is also it. There they say 'That's it, that's not' from one point of view, here we say 'That's it, that's not' from another point of view. Are there really It and Other? Or really no It and Other? Where neither It nor Other finds its opposite is called axis of the Way."[25]

Interpreting this passage, one can say, Otherness then is not the opposite of that which *Is*, but rather the other side of the *Is*. The Is is both the Is and the Is Not. Is and Is Not are parts of the Way. The Is is the other and the Other is the Is. The way is precisely the simple, indivisible, and indestructible present in everything that is and is not, that is not and is.

Chuang Tzu does not abide by the Aristotelean law of non-contradiction that something is and is not. It either is or is not. Chuang Tzu, on the other hand, argues that the Way embraces both the Is and the Is Not simultaneously, that one can assert both at the same time. Otherness is essentially beyond the absolutes of the principle of non contradiction.

For him, that Is implies that it is also Is Not, or that something is not is also that which is. Something Is, is just a certain person's opinion just like something is not is but another person's opinion. These two opinions are integral aspects of the dynamic flow of the Way.

Given these premises, the Self's sex, gender, and race are also part of the Way, as the Way constructs paths of being for the Self. Thus, the Self is a man, is not a man; is a woman, is not a woman; is both, and is not both are all constructions of the Way. The Way is not a simple entity; it is, rather, a composite of possibilities, inherently changing appearances.

Another passage enforces the above view, "The Way has never had borders, saying has never had norms. It is by a 'That is it which deems that a boundary is marked . . . to "divide"' then is to leave something undivided."[26]

The establishment of the norms of sex, gender, and race is inherently discriminatory. The labels themselves are boundaries and limitations of the paths of the Self, the paths of the Way, or the paths of the Egyptian Nun.

NOTES

15. Baird and Heimbeck, *Asian Philosophy*, 304.
16. Ibid., 392.
17. Ibid., 393.
18. Ibid., 393.
19. Ibid., 421.

20. Ibid., 422.
21. Kant, Immanuel, and Norman Kemp Smith, *Immanuel Kant's Critique of Pure Reason* (Boston: Bedford, 1929).
22. Ibid., 424.
23. Ibid., 424.
24. Ibid., 426.
25. Ibid., 416.
26. Ibid., 419.

• 5 •

Buddhist Innovations

  The Buddha does not engage with metaphysical speculations in the same manner as all the philosophical traditions that were examined above. Rather, he takes the binaries of the tradition into which he was born and extends profound respect to the appearances of the Self, by advocating that all selves make concerted efforts to remove human suffering by practicing the Eightfold Path. The Eightfold Path is composed of right understanding, right contemplation, right conduct, right effort, right vocation, right vigilance, right thought, and right aspiration. The effort is on the rightness of the choices that one makes in light of the uniqueness of the individual who chooses the correct paths toward enlightenment.

  The self must seek enlightenment. Enlightenment itself has four characteristics. One: it is like a mirror free of images. Two: it is truly non-empty, which means it embraces all objects free of destruction. Three: it is like a clean mirror free of dirt. Four: because it is clean, it can purify all other minds.[27] This is known as *Suchness*. Such is purity and simplicity.

  In direct contrast, unenlightenment has the following characteristics. One: it is the activity of ignorance. Two: because it is agitated, it is a perceiving subject. Three: it perceives appearances. Four: its distorted perceptions produce six aspects, which are, (1) develops likes and dislikes, (2) is subject to pain and pleasure, (3) attachment is cultivated, (4) it is guided by incomplete concepts of a denuded mind, (5) a denuded mind is attached to evil, and (6) it is subject to anxiety, fear, and suffering.

  Suchness, a state of bliss, Self, and purity, refreshing coolness, immutability, and freedom can be attained by the practice of meditation and the perfection of faith. Faith is attained through the practice of straightforwardness, profundity, and compassion. A repeated practice of the above will inevitably open the gateway to Suchness. Faith is strengthened further when the seeker meditates on the dignity of all beings, the avoidance of evil, the practice of goodness, and the great vow of universal salvation.[28] Practices for the perfection of faith involve charity, observance of precepts, patience, zeal, cessation of illusion, and clear observation. These are the secrets of Suchness—open to all selves free of race, sex, and gender.

Under ideal conditions, Suchness as a realization of enlightenment is a possibility for all selves and is not determined by race, sex, and gender. Suchness is a possibility for the Self that desires goodness, compassion, the conquest of evil, and the salvation of human kind.

Many are called to this ideal, but few arrive at the summit. The rest dangle in the middle, lost, anxious, anguished, and ignorant, knowing neither what to do nor how to do it, nor what they think they should do. These are the unenlightened, and they have not embarked on the open path of Suchness, the quest for perfection, as Sri Aurobindo said.

NOTES

27. Kant, Immanuel, and Norman Kemp Smith, *Immanuel Kant's Critique of Pure Reason* (Boston: Bedford, 1929), 468.

28. Ibid., 482.

· 6 ·

The Self in Greek Thought

A. PLATO

*P*lato and Aristotle absorb pre-Socratic thoughts, which originated in Egypt and were then appropriated by Thales and Pythagoras before reappearing in an original form in the writings of Plato, and later Aristotle.[29] Plato and Aristotle analyze some of these pre-Socratic arguments in their later works. Plato discusses the Pythagorean ideas in his dialogues, and Aristotle discusses Parmenides extensively in his *Metaphysics*. The pre-Socratics, which proudly remember their indebtedness to their Egyptian teachers, are equally proudly interpreted and appropriated by Plato and Aristotle in all their published texts.

In *The Symposium*[30] as well as in *The Republic* and *The Laws*, Plato addresses the meaning of love and then indirectly addresses the status of appearances, such as sex and gender.

The Self's nature is analyzed at a drinking party through the lens of several philosophers' characterization of love in Plato's famous work *The Symposium*. The Self in *The Symposium* is defined in multiple ways, showing the complexities of the Self's sexual orientation and styles of existence.

Several philosophers, including Socrates, at a dinner party in a joyous mood, reflect on the meaning of love, and the result is a meandering discourse that does not aim at a singular understanding of love, but rather a labyrinth of forms, providing the reader with a rich vision of the possibilities of being a human in love.

In *The Symposium*, the lover is presented as a complex person without a singular sex or gender. The lover exemplifies possibilities of Being.

Thus, begins Phaedrus, love, is the oldest of the gods. So wise is love, that young lovers who are attracted to one another are the better for it. Most particularly, young boys would be the beneficiaries of this virtuous love, this rational love. Right here in the very beginning, Phaedrus is endorsing heterosexual love, naturally and casually, and thus emerges the first definition of a gay sexual orientation. Men and women would die for such a love. This is a divinely inspired love, for which male and female lovers will give their lives. These young lovers are attracted to the virtues of the older and wiser lover. The lover is not responding to physical form, however, tempting as that might be. This is a spiritual and rational love. The intelligent one is not tempted by the love of the body but the love of the soul, the soul of the divinely inspired older lover.

Pausanias speaks next. He immediately notes that there are many kinds of love and sets out to correct Phaedrus's praise of one kind of love. He argues that love is inseparable from Aphrodite—and as there are two goddesses, there must also be two loves. He calls them Heavenly Love and Common Love. The older goddess is heavenly, the other goddess, is common. The common type of love is wanton and undiscriminating. Both men and women are subject to it. Heavenly Love is rational and discriminating, and is attracted to male lovers and female lovers, provided that they are intelligent. This love is attracted to intelligence in any sex. Commitment is its cardinal attribute. Deliberation is its leading form. Sustenance is its inner shell. This love would commit itself to the beloved for the course of a life. Such is the nature of Heavenly Love. Common Love is fleeting and impermanent and moves with the whims of desire while acting impetuously. These two kinds of love must be united and give birth to a third kind of love. The third kind of love is homosexuality and lesbianism—new forms of love.

Finally, Socrates presents his view of love, which is the longest and most complicated speech on the subject. For Socrates, following Diotima, who he says is his teacher, love is neither divine nor mortal but in the middle of the two. Love is a daimon, a supernatural force, which partakes in the nature of divinity and super humanity, but it is not as divine as Phaedrus idealizes it to be. Love is in the middle, and it partakes in the nature of the good and the nature of the bad. Love is an interpreter between gods and humans. God interacts with humans through the interpretations of love. Love brings God to humans and humans interact with God through love. Love is the son of the gods Plenty and Poverty, born to a drunken Plenty and poor Poverty. This is a tale which Socrates tells, as an account of Love's birth.

Love was born on the birthdate of Aphrodite, the goddess who gave the feast at which Poros (Plenty), as a guest, was heavily drunk. So, Love, who is beautiful, is a follower of Aphrodite, since he was conceived at her birthday party. Love is always poor, (like his mother), and a strong, enterprising, mighty hunter, and always philosophical, (traits he took from his father). That is why

Love is not mortal or immortal, but plenty and flourishing, like his father, Plenty. Love is always in the mean, neither rich nor poor, nor knowledgeable, nor ignorant, but in the middle.

God does not seek knowledge, because he already knows. Love however is not a god. Love, as a mean, necessarily seeks knowledge, since he is partly ignorant but wishes to know. Love, therefore, is a philosopher. Love, in part, is beautiful because it is attracted to philosophy, because philosophy as an expression of wisdom is beautiful. As Socrates puts it, "For Wisdom is a most beautiful thing, and Love is of the beautiful; and therefore, Love is also a philosopher or lover of wisdom."[31] Love is also attracted to evil, to transgression, and to the violation of norms and distortion of values.

Love is also a quest for immortality. Since it is a mean between the mortal and the non-mortal, it is always seeking its other half. For this, Love seeks by generation to make itself immortal. Love experiences generation as a quest for eternity and immortality. Immortality is a kind of good, which humans seek to possess. The search for immortality, then, is a search for the possession of the good itself and the blending of the good and the beautiful.

The quest for immortality was first articulated in Egypt, a quest from which Plato draws approvingly and proudly, for which we must admire him. Plato brilliantly appropriates this Egyptian insight and makes it his intimate own. He hones it.

Love always begotten by generation seeks to leave traces of the beautiful as a mark of its existence. The reproduction of the species is a potent example of the quest for immortality as the project of Love. When the body dies, Love seeks immortality by maintaining a pure soul, which is deathless, therefore immortal.[32] Immortality is, therefore, sought after by generation, and when the body, which begets generation, dies, it is pursued by the immortality of the soul. The body, which is mortal, seeks to immortalize itself by birthing children; and the soul, which is pregnant with wisdom, becomes immortal and preserves its spiritual beauty through deathlessness.

Love, in the end, is a contemplation of the beautiful—which is non-bodily—the mortal part of what Love seeks as it yearns for immortality and joins the beautiful souls who are deathless. The body can encounter these deathless souls only in death. That is why true love is a contemplation of the beautiful and therefore good itself, which is embodied in the deathless soul. Immortality, as the practice of dying, is the philosopher's enduring quest. It is the ultimate search for truth, but the body must first die in order for this quest to be realized as the consummation of the life well lived, and well ended—at least temporally and spatially—since the self is temporal and spatial.

Socrates praises Diotima, his wise female teacher, and concludes, "that Life above all others which man should live, in the contemplation of beauty absolute; a beauty which if you once beheld, you would see not to be after the measure of gold, and garments, and fair boys and youths, whose presence now entrances you; and you and many a one would be content to live seeing them only and conversing with them without meat or drink, if that were possible—you only want to look at them and to be with them. But what if what man had eyes to see the true beauty—the divine beauty, I mean, pure and clear and unalloyed, not clogged with the pollutions of mortality and all the colors and vanities of human life, thither looking, and holding converse with the true beauty simple and divine?"[33]

With this question, Socrates explores the limitations of appearances, race, gender, and sex as nothing more than the contingent languages of the mortal part of love, whereas the non-mortal part is divine and pregnant with the non-mortal and non-material ontology of Being. Love is the ultimate expression of infinite possibilities, in the form of the practice of dying to the body and waking to the soul.

Being is beyond race, gender, and sex and the contemplation of beauty is a yearning for uniting with Being, which does not need these blinding forces of the mortal side of love. By this brilliant move Plato, following Socrates, who in turn is educated by a woman, takes us beyond the corrupting and limiting mortal condition to the radically new zone of Being. Central to this project is the education of Love, which is pursued in *The Republic*, a work of the elderly philosopher.

In *The Republic*,[34] sex and gender again are indirectly addressed through an examination of the human Soul. The Soul is neither male nor female. It is only human, the essence of the ontology of Being, and that is precisely what Plato carefully dissects. In *The Republic*, we are treated to a brilliantly articulated ontology of Being as such.

The soul does not have a sex and gender. It is analyzed as a simple and indestructible thing that is composed of three aspects: reason, spirit, and desire. Reason guides spirit and desire. Spirit is always inclined to act, and follows the whims of desire. Reason, fully conscious of the nature of spirit and desire, intervenes to provide the much-needed guidance. When spirit and desire willingly submit to reason's guidance, a well-ordered and harmonious soul is the result. The Soul thus examined is the human soul, with possibilities of choice in the realms of sexual and gender orientations. Plato's intent is to examine a single and simple soul without binaries. The harmonious soul chooses styles of existence and ways of being. Sex and gender are consequences of choices that the harmonious soul chooses. Plato examines the nature of the soul, not separate male and female souls. He is concerned with the structure of the human soul, as he prepares his vision of the perfect city—the city of well-ordered souls.

Once the soul is carefully studied, it becomes the ground for the ideal city he builds, based on the ontological principle of equality that informs the relationship between males and females, females and females, and males and males depending on the sexualities and genders that they consciously choose with an awareness of the nature of their individual souls. Plato trusts human beings to make the right choices, once they alertly examine the conditions of their souls and how well ordered they are. Sexual orientations and gendered cultures are informed by the conditions of the soul. Given the conditions, correct choices inevitably follow.

The ideal city of *The Republic* is inhabited by citizens whose souls are carefully nurtured and can be trusted to make the right choices in the realms of sexual orientation and gendered lifestyles.

This theme is analyzed again in *The Laws*.

B. ARISTOTLE

In direct contrast to Plato, and reminiscent of Confucius's binary world, not to mention a radical departure from the Egyptian sex-neutral gaze, where sex and gender are dogmatically assumed to be parts of the anatomical order of the world and uncritical of tradition, Aristotle defends the tyranny of tradition and argues that men and women are not only anatomically different but also intellectually and morally different.

Again, like Confucius before him, Aristotle cultivates a world inhabited by men and women with different places in society. Men are chosen as potential gentlemen, and women are the dependent appendages who do not exist for themselves.

Although he begins at the right place, when he asserts that the distinguishing characteristic of the human, in contrast to animals and plants, is thinking, he does not consistently extend this capacity to women. He thinks that men think and women feel; men govern and women are ruled; men run the political world and women manage the household; men earn money and women administer it; men fight in battles and women raise children. Men are autonomous persons whose essence it thinking, and women are emotional beings whose essence is feeling and changing their minds.

He reserves the capacity of thinking for men. For him, thinking is a male activity, and feeling in the form of compassion, empathy, tearing easily, and mischief is characteristically female. The rational principle is distinctly male; it is the virtue that qualifies the male to rule over women and slaves who are not endowed with this capacity.[35]

The Aristotelean world is ordered by men. Women quietly assume their assigned place. In this world women and slaves occupy the same space, one of submission and unrecognized labor. His world is a world of inequality and submission to the passions and needs of men. Women are born to make their mates great. They are born not to rule but to be ruled, not to order but to obey, not to create but to manage a world created by men. They are meant to be economists of the household, not of nations and empires.

To make matters worse, for Aristotle, race, sex, and gender are governed by natural conventions. Thus, by natural convention, some women and men are natural slaves. There are those persons who are born to be slaves and are not capable of ruling their lives. They must be ruled by men, particularly by men who are natural rulers. They are born to serve others. Anatomically, women are not only different from men, but their very structure marks them as subservient to men. Women, in his view, enjoy serving men—very much like slaves enjoy obeying their masters.

A passage from Aristotle's *Politics* shows this to be the case: "again, the relation of male to female is naturally that of the superior to the inferior—of the ruling to the ruled." He likens this to the relation of the soul to the body, in which the soul rules the body.[36]

NOTES

29. Martin Heidegger interprets some pre-Socratic fragments in *What is Called Thinking* and also in *Metaphysics*.
30. Stephen David Ross (ed), *Art and Its Significance* (New York: New York State University Press, 1984).
31. Ibid., 58.
32. Plato, *Plato's Phaedo* (Oxford, UK: Clarendon Press, 1911).
33. Ibid., 63.
34. Ibid., 31–44.
35. Aristotle, *Aristotle's Politics* (Oxford, UK: Clarendon Press, 1905).
36. Ibid., 13.

· 7 ·

Race, Sex, and Gender in the Quran

𝓘n the Quran it says,

> Tell the believing men to lower their gaze and to be mindful of their chastity: this will be most conducive to their purity—(and,) verily, Allah is aware of all that they do. And tell the believing women to lower their gaze and to be mindful of their chastity, and not to display their charms beyond what may be apparent thereof; hence let them draw their veils over their bosoms and do not show their adornments except to their husbands or their fathers or their husbands' fathers or their sons or their husbands' sons or their brothers or their brothers' sons or their sisters' sons or their women or what their right hands possess or male servants free of sexual desires or those children who never know the private things of women; and do not stamp their feet so that it may show their hidden adornments; and repent towards God collectively O believers so that you may succeed.
>
> —Quran, Sura 24 (An-Nur), ayat 27–31

These are classical passages and the arguments they establish are quite clear. Men and women are really not equal, but women can still attend mosques in spite of the inequality. Women are sufficiently equal to men to stand or sit next to men at mosques. But, women and men are partitioned by curtains at mosques, so that men will not see the women's bodies. This act considerably reduces the idea of equality. In the name of protection, the possibilities of self-definition are severely limited. Curtains, like walls, separate humans from free interaction with one another, (as is deemed necessary), and enforce self-imposed boundaries regarding what men and women should and should not share. The Imams should not give this power to themselves; they should leave it to others to define their own possibilities and ways of life.

The passage does not mention race, gender, or sex. It does try to protect women from the intrusive male gaze—the gaze that reduces women to their bodily parts—by advising women to not exhibit their body parts for the male's enjoyment. Some modern women may appreciate this protection. Others, who would like to freely move with their bodies, may consider the protection a curtailment of their freedoms. They in fact may prefer to live in regimes in which they can go about with their bodies as they so choose.

The race of these women is not mentioned. It is as if the protection is race neutral. If that is the case, then the argument is originally powerful and Islam's greatness must be acknowledged.

· 8 ·

The Self in the Enlightenment Thinkers

A. ZARA YACOB

With the rise of the Enlightenment, a powerful African voice found a vision of the enlightened self from the northern highlands of Ethiopia. His name was Zara Yacob. Having come before the European voices of the Enlightenment—such as Descartes from France and Kant from Germany, who were popularized as the founders of the Enlightenment—I dub Zara Yacob the African voice of the Global project of Enlightenment.[37]

Historically and intellectually, it is Zara Yacob who was the first to systematically articulate the idea of the Enlightenment. Some scholars would say he is the founder of Afro modernity. I prefer to simply say that Zara Yacob is the founder of modernity, as a moment of Enlightenment.

Zara Yacob, like Confucius and Aristotle before him, uncritically internalizes the binaries male/female, man/woman and proceeds to define them through the lens of religion. He is a religious thinker, critical of organized religion, but not sufficiently critical of the oppressive binaries of sex and gender. However, like Plato before him, and unlike Confucius and Aristotle, Zara Yacob does not think that women are inferior to men. On the contrary, he thinks that women and men are deeply equal intellectually and spiritually.

Zara Yacob's comments on sex and gender are very sparse, yet however few they are, their content is extraordinarily respectful of women, in the tradition of Plato.

Here is a typical passage, "All men are equal in the presence of God, and all are intelligent since they are his creatures, he did not assign one for life, another for death; one for mercy and another for judgement. Our reason teaches us that this sort of discrimination cannot exist in the sight of God, who is perfect in all his works."[38]

The potential application of this enlightenment proposition to the human condition is vast. From the passage we can draw the thesis that the binaries themselves are founded on God's commands—provided that we do not play one sex against another—and that sex and gender are founded on the principle of nondiscrimination, since all humans are equal in the eyes of God. By this measure, the practice of any discrimination is a violation of God's laws. God's laws command categorically that human life is sacrosanct and that the existential rights of humans cannot be violated. In this view the children of God can choose any sexual orientation that fulfills them, and their creator who knows them will cultivate their choices, and not arbitrarily obstruct their paths.

Humans must exercise existential seriousness in the treatment of others. There are no others who can be abused or treated indifferently. To do so is to abuse their creator, namely God himself.

In principle then, Zara Yacob can be expected to go beyond the binaries of men and women, male and female, and recognize the diversity of human desires, provided that they are not discriminatory. Zara Yacob is fully prepared to reject tradition and custom if they are premised on unreasonable treatment of human beings, particularly in the relationships between men and women. Unlike Aristotle, who believed that women are inferior to men, Zara Yacob argues that men and women are equal in the presence of God. They are both endowed with the power of reason. He argues that the capacity of thinking is gender and race neutral, a truly explosive thesis coming out of the seventeenth century.

It is his demand that humans exercise their God-given intelligence at all times and in all situations that makes him the founder of Afro-modernity, as some people insist, and the original voice of the Enlightenment, as I prefer to call him.

B. DESCARTES

Descartes,[39] like Zara Yacob before him, argues that what is distinctive about humans is that they are thinking beings who are equipped with a reasoning power. It is this proposition that makes Zara Yacob and Descartes the founders of the Enlightenment project, and the voices of the Global South and the Global North, respectively. Reason anchors itself in Africa and Europe, as these two original minds dig deep into the inner lives of thinking beings, that is, human beings.

Descartes grounds human equality in the power of a God given reason. When we use reason correctly we uncover the fact that sex and gender are only appearances, which often lead them to battle one another. When we uncover the existence of reason, we learn that neither sex is inferior to another, and that the sexes and genders are in fact equal. Battling need not have any place in this venture, but a free expression of what the self feels would be the better place to begin.

As Cecile Alduy put it,

> Forget Simone de Beauvoir, Betty Friedan, and Naomi Wolf. Descartes gave us all that we needed to claim gender equality a long time ago. Historians rarely remember it this way, but women's rights were dramatically (if hypothetically) advanced when, in 1619, René Descartes, snow-bound in a stove-heated room in Neuberg, Germany, had the crazy idea to bet that the body might be entirely an illusion of the senses. But—and how cool is this—when "I" am thinking that very thought, "I" must exist, therefore "I" am. And this "I" is a thinking thing ("cogito ergo sum and sum res cogitans"). Now, Descartes was too busy with the Existence of God argument to spell out the full consequences of this simple fact for the so-called weaker sex, but, had he looked into it, the old man would have agreed that this "I" defined by Reason alone is necessarily gender neutral (no body, no sex, right?). Or, as French philosopher Elisabeth Badinter puts it in What Is A Woman?, ontologically speaking, "a woman is a man like any other."[40]

Alduy is right. There is much that we can draw from this proposition about the status of sex and gender. To do full justice to Descartes I must summarize the arguments of *The Meditations*, in which Descartes proves by reasoning that humans are thinking things.

In the *First Meditation*, Descartes makes a case for the possibility of removing himself from his body, while he is still thinking. Whereas he could remove his body at will, he cannot do so with the mind, which leads to the *Second Meditation*, in which he now knows that he is a thinking thing, a thinking thing who must necessarily exist in order to even doubt that he does not exist. The doubter—one who thinks that he could remove his body—must exist in order to doubt that he might not exist.

This move conveniently enabled Descartes, in the *Third Meditation*, to ask the question, now that he knows he exists as a thinking thing: who is the cause of this thinking thing who exists?

He considers several possibilities and finds all of them, with the exception of the last one, unconvincing: (1) He knows that he is not the cause of his existence, and that (2) He was caused by another more perfect being. In addition, (3) he has always existed, and certainly, (4) His parents caused his existence. (5) He must therefore have been caused to exist, or have been created, by a perfect Being, and this Being can only be God.

He now proceeds, in the *Fourth Meditation*, to argue that when he makes mistakes it is only his imperfect will that causes him to make those mistakes.

In the *Fifth Meditation*, he describes God as infinitely perfect, so perfect that he has the capacity to create himself and other persons as thinking things.

In the *Sixth Meditation,* he argues that God can do anything. He can make us see all that He has created, clearly and distinctly. He can create us as thoughts who could exist without bodies, or bodies who could exist without thoughts. Descartes therefore concludes that he could exist as thought without a body, or a body without thought, as he concluded in the *First Meditation*.

All these arguments are waged on the behalf of the human self and are not distinct designations of either men or women. For Descartes, the attribute of thinking belongs to human beings, in a sex and gender neural modality of existence. Descartes is developing an ontology of human existence.[41]

We can draw several arguments about self-definition from Descartes. First, the thinking self can, given the empowering attribute of thinking, think for itself and construct values and norms that authenticate its lifestyle, such as the sex and gender that fit its choices.

Second, women in particular, who are otherwise treated as servile, are redefined as part and parcel of the thinking self, born as men's equals, and capable of legislating for themselves and the world.

Third, women are not peculiar beings who feel without thinking. They are, instead, universal, thinking beings, who think and feel, and who feel and think.

Fourth, closely following Zara Yacob, the founder of modernity, Descartes gives a portrait of women as endowed with reason and born as the equals of men. Together, Zara Yacob and Descartes give women a forum from which they can battle centuries of oppressive European masculine gaze with the equalizing gaze of reason.

C. KANT

Kant is also wedded to the binary traditions into which he was born. He did not transcend them the way Plato, Zara Yacob, and Descartes did. More like Aristotle, Kant is not respectful of women and Africans, both of whom are naturally inferior to white men. His personal opinions about women are in sharp contrast to his metaphysics, as articulated in his moral philosophy, *Foundations of the Metaphysics of Morals*, in which he gives a rich understanding of the human, in the manner of Zara Yacob and Descartes.

For Kant, as well as Zara Yacob and Descartes before him, the human is equipped with a reasoning power, which empowers the person to make correct moral decisions, or undertake morally worthy actions.

For Kant, the cornerstone of the morally worthy action is the fact that it is guided by a good will, and the willing itself must necessarily be good. The necessary component of the will is the good itself. Drawing from his categories of reason, we can surmise that the modality of the will must be necessarily good, and that necessity is one of the subcategories of modality. Happiness, at which all willing aims, must necessarily be anchored in goodness itself, being that willing is authentic only when it is good, and something is good because the willing itself is.

As Kant puts it, "The first proposition of morality is that to have genuine moral worth, an action must be done from duty . . . the third principle is that Duty is the necessity to do an action from respect for Law."[42]

Duty is the application of good will. Morally worthy action guided by the will inevitably leads one to choose correctly. The moral subject is instructed that he must choose dutifully, and that this dutifulness is a categorical imperative, which is one of reason's categories, the category of relation. Dutiful actions, therefore, command categorically. The categorical imperative, distinct from the hypothetical imperative, is guided by respect for the moral law that cannot be transgressed unless the moral subject has lost his anchor in the reason of the moral law, which commands categorically and not hypothetically.

One example of duty that is exemplary as a categorical imperative is, "The practical imperative. . . . Act so that you treat Humanity whether in your own person or in that of another, always as an end and never as a means only."[43]

From this imperative, we can draw several possibilities of how to rethink the moral status of the appearances of race, sex, and gender in inventive ways.

It is at the sight of men and women's interactions as humans with the same ontological structure that the moral status is understood as a categorical imperative, for which Kant could have argued they are expected to be respected as ends, whose dignities and existential rights cannot be violated. The imperative demands further that we cannot abuse, exploit, or mistreat any human being. To do so is to violate the conditions of the imperative. Freedom cannot be denied to any human person, such as women, homosexuals, or other future possibilities. The morally worthy action, or public policy, must be informed by this stringent imperative.

Kant's personal view on women is itself contradicted by the categorical imperative that he has brilliantly articulated. This imperative could also be extended to the sphere of labor, on which Marx feasted when he developed his sophisticated labor theory of value premised on exploitation at the point of production. Women and men are both brutally exploited in this sphere, and this exploitation could be stopped categorically by the actions of the exploited themselves, fully armed with Kant's classic categorical imperative that unconditionally condemns the abuse of human dignity, including exploitation of labor in the workplace, where goods are produced, consumed, distributed, and sold. The categorical imperative also protects race, sexuality, and gender from the process of commodification.

Against Kant's compliance with capitalist exploitation, his own categorical imperative protests against him.

D. HEGEL

I will begin with the following to introduce Hegel's views on race, sex, and gender. I fully concur with Jane Dryden that:

> For a feminist philosopher like me, who has an ongoing interest in and concern with Hegel's thought, the more troubling criticisms come from feminist philosophers who have worked through the details and implications of his system as a whole. For example, Alison Stone argues that gendered opposition within Hegel's philosophy is not merely confined to his discussion of the family; rather, gendered opposition is deeply embedded in Hegel's system, in his very understanding of nature, and the relationship of concept and matter (Stone 2010, 212–3). Since Hegel associates form or concept with the male and matter with the female, in common with most of the Western philosophical tradition, his identification of matter as the "being-outside-itself of the concept" means Hegel "implicitly understands the female as the being-outside-itself of the male—as an inverted and inferior form of the male, rather than as a sexual identity in its own right." Thus, Hegel's account of the process of nature, where the concept shapes matter more and more in conformity with it, "amounts to a progressive mastery of the female by the male" (212; emphasis in Stone). That this account is deeply embedded in Hegel's thinking means that it is not possible to strategically bracket gender to the side and to continue to use other aspects of his philosophy. Furthermore, the character of this account also raises troubling questions, more generally, about the role of contingency in Hegel.[44]

Like Kant before him, Hegel also develops a philosophy of the Self that treats it as a historically evolving consciousness that matures in the womb of time and creates suitable spaces for this unfolding to occur. Hegel's foremost project is to allow humans to become conscious historical subjects, certainly born to nature with definite anatomy, but evolving cultural beings. Hegel correctly notes that anatomy is not destiny, in fact, anatomy is potentiality. Anatomy is an actuality that becomes potentiality. In this sense, the Self is an evolving actuality heading toward self-realization in history. The Self is, furthermore, historical growth.

In this vast sense, race, sex, sexuality, and gender are not static natural givens but historical possibilities. Hegel, unlike Kant, inserts human possibilities into history, in which the human lives inside nature but also inside history. Both nature, of which anatomy is a definite part, and history, which is an evolving actuality, are impregnated with possibilities. Nature and history are incubating in the womb of time and space. The self is a temporal and historical being.

Temporality, spatiality, and historicity become attributes of the Self. In this view, race, sex, sexuality, and gender are temporal, spatial, and historical. Therefore, the fully conscious historical self can choose its race, sex, sexuality, and gender in the course of maturing and growing with nature and inside history. The self must fight for these rights by creating institutions of civil society, and most particularly, an efficient State that recognizes these styles of existence.

The conscious self can fight for the appearances that it chooses, as a matter of historical and natural right. For Hegel, appearances are real but they have not actualized yet. They are raw givens. Race, sex, and gender are also themselves raw actualities. They have not fully consummated their potential. The self finds these appearances in time and space and uncritically inhabits them by prematurely making them its own, without critically and consciously examining their ontological status as it finds them in the world.

Hegel's Phenomenology is one powerful articulation of this thesis through the brilliant concept of recognition. In a deeper sense, the struggle for recognition is fundamentally an attempt at self-definition, an attempt by the Self to consciously articulate and live styles of existence and an ethics of living. The quest for recognition is simultaneously a strategic yearning for the existence of a rational and spiritual state that treats the human with the tools of Kant's categorical imperative embodied in the institutions of civil society and the constitution of the State. The categorical imperative is that the world is consciously made by human labor. The world belongs to those who tilled it and who must own the products, an insight that Marx inherited and developed in his theory of alienation in *The Economic and Philosophical Manuscripts of 1844*, then carried it further to *Capital*, in which he provides an original theory of exploitation at the point of production.

Hegel mentions women only in three places in *The Phenomenology*. In one of them, Hegel writes, "The feminine element, therefore, in the form of the sister, premonizes and foreshadows most completely the nature of ethical life. She does not become conscious of it, and does not actualize it, because the law of the family is her inherent implicit inward nature, which does not lie open to the daylight of consciousness but remains an inner feeling and the divine element exempt from actuality. The feminine life is attached to these household divinities (Penates), and sees in them both her universal substance, and her particular individuality, yet so views them that this relation of her individuality to them is at the same time not the natural one of pleasure."[45]

Again, "The union of man and woman constitutes the operative mediating agency for the whole, and constitutes the element which, while separated into the extremes of divine and human law, is at the same time, their immediate union."[46]

Finally, "Womankind-the everlasting irony in the life of the community—changes by intrigue the universal purpose of government into a private end, transforms its universal activity into a work of this or that specific individual, and perverts the universal property of the state into a possession and ornament for the family. Woman in this way turns to ridicule the grave wisdom of maturity . . . to private pleasure, personal satisfaction . . . she makes this wisdom the laughing stock of raw and wanton youth."[47]

These passages speak for themselves. They express profound disrespect for women. Their historically imposed roles within the family in which they sculpt the character of children is relegated to irrelevance, as part of nature. The real work of recognition is assigned to men as they assert their individuality as the founders of the rational state. They fight for their freedom, whereas women exist only as supplements to men as they are being cultivated to be gentlemen, as Confucius before Hegel, and Kant after Hegel, long argued.

For Hegel individuality and freedom are the attributes of men, and domesticity and feeling are feminine attributes. Self-consciousness cannot be attained by women because they are preoccupied in the family sphere.

Hegel betrays his own powerful vision of the Self as a historical moral/political subject, and insensitively removes women from this emancipated space and relegates them to selves without personality or actionability.

E. KIERKEGAARD

Kierkegaard's view of sex, sexuality, and gender is discussed in the context of love. For him, the woman is fundamentally an embodiment of the beautiful. A passage from *Either/Or* (1843) brings this out most clearly, when he writes, "My eyes can never weary of surveying this peripheral manifold, these scattered emanations of feminine beauty. Each particular has its little share and yet is complete in itself, happy, glad, beautiful. Every woman has her share: the merry smile, the roguish smile, the yearning look . . . Then my soul is glad, my heart beats, my passion is aflame. This one woman, the only woman in the world, she must belong to me, she must be mine. Let God keep heaven, if I could keep her."[48]

With these passionate words, Kierkegaard accepts the woman as a relationship with God. It is God who chose the woman to be an eternal partner of man, his very equal. By creating her as beautiful, God prepares her for a man's soul. It is her particular gifts, which Kierkegaard describes with extraordinary sensitivity, to which man is attracted. For Kierkegaard, man and woman are different, with different endowments, which command categorical respect founded on the principle of maximum equality. Some feminists might correctly find that these portraits of women objectify women as a background for masculine desire, which they might argue is disempowering. They are right, because there are no corresponding physical descriptions of men, since men are recognized only as intellectual and spiritual beings.

Sadly, his description of man's qualities is not as descriptive and as complete as those of women. However, in his eyes, man and woman are absolute equals in the presence of God. Man and woman are the ultimate synthesis, one man for one woman, chosen by God. It is God who chooses and cultivates this relation of body and soul. It is God who chooses a fitting partner for man. Of course, Kierkegaard implicitly assumes that it is God who gave men and women the physical and spiritual qualities they possess, and that his duty is to describe the reality that God has created. If these descriptions are sexist, it is a sexism that God has created with his mystical reasoning that the believer must submit to, as this is the nature of faith.

This spiritual relation is further examined in *Works of Love*. Humans are challenged in this essay to love God and their neighbors. These are absolute commands, which cannot be violated. The love of man and woman is also anchored in these commands. *Neighbor* implies all of God's children. Man and woman are expected to love each other more than they love themselves individually. They are a unity and this unity is founded on neighborly love. Their unity is chosen by God. It is a duty commanded by God that they love each other unconditionally. Commitment is the expression of this love, as God intended it.

Love itself is a duty. This love is eternal although practiced temporally. Its expressions must be free of jealousy, and most importantly, of despair. The love of woman and man should not despair when unhappiness strikes because unhappiness is part of the human condition, which in due time will be attended to by God. Lovers must patiently wait for this unhappiness to pass.

No condition is permanent. If this observation of human life is correct, then the negative dimensions of life, of which the unhappiness with which life is impregnated, challenge us to patiently wait without despair. Despair denies that no condition is permanent, and it sometimes leads to suicide, when what is needed is to patiently wait for despair to pass.

Waiting is the final cure for despair. Kierkegaard was profoundly aware of this phenomenon that he links with the fear of death, or what Heidegger, following Kierkegaard, dubbed as one of the central fears of *Dasein* (existence), the fear of death.

NOTES

37. Teodros Kiros, *Zara Yabob: Rationality of the Human Heart* (Trenton, NJ: Red Sea Press, 2005).

38. Adeshina Afalayan and Toyin Falola, eds, *The Palgrave Handbook of African Philosophy* (London: Palgrave MacMillan, 2017), 199.

39. Descartes, *Discourse On Method and Meditations* (London:: MacMillan, 1952), 61–126.

40. Cecile Alduy, "The Philosopher, the Mother and the Baby," *Arcade: Literature, the Humanities & the World*, Stanford University, August 25, 2012, https://arcade.stanford.edu/blogs/philosopher-mother-and-baby.

41. Descartes, *Discourse on Method and Meditations*.

42. Emmanuel Kant, *Foundations of the Metaphysics of Morals* (Upper Saddle River, NJ: Prentice Hall, 1997), 16.

43. Ibid., 46.

44. Jane Dryden, "Hegel, Feminist Philosophy, and Disability: Rereading our History," *Disability Studies Quarterly* 33, no. 4 (2013).

45. G.W.E Hegel, *The Phenomenology of Mind* (New York: Harper Torch Books, 1967), 176.

46. Ibid., 482.

47. Ibid., 496.

48. Soren Kierkegaard, *A Kierkegaard Anthology*, edited by Robert Bretall (New York: Modern Library Books, 1936), 72.

Part II

· 9 ·

Modernity and the Sexed and Gendered Bodies

A. HEIDEGGER

Heidegger's references to sex, sexuality, and gender are almost nonexistent, but they can be inferred from his characterization of *Dasein* (existence), which is race, sex and gender neutral. He also does not mention women in the context of his reflections on Being outside what he says about Dasein, which is sex neutral. It refers to the *there*, and the *there* is all those humans in the world and of the world. The *they* are *there*. Men, women, and others are integral parts of Being there in the World. They are part of the dynamic nature of being beyond the static facticity of the anatomical structure of Being, the presentness of sex, as opposed to gender, which is transcendental, the ever-evolving possibility of Dasein.

In *Being and Time*, Heidegger carefully develops the analysis of Dasein, as that projection to the future and reflection of the past, both of which are modalities of presence, which Heidegger explodes. Dasein as the there and now is present, and it also points to the future, having already been in the past. Dasein is at once past, present, and future. As the present it has an anatomy and a biological structure. That is its ontic structure. It is at the same time beyond the present, as it projects into the future. That is its ontological structure as a possibility, a transcendence.

Being as sex and gender is a neutral term that can be analyzed factually, as that which is present in time and history, readily understood through its biology, and transcendentally, as that which has multiple possibilities. Its factual beingness is taken for granted by the they, because the they confer existence and values to Being, uncritically. The ontic is considered to be Being's final existence in its utmost concretion. Heidegger the philosopher, however, seeks to go beyond the veil of the present but must necessarily begin with a description of the ontic, a description of biology, of sex, which he then transcends with the disclosure of Being and its transcendental possibilities, such as gender. Gender, like sex, has also an ontic existence conferred on Being by the they. Heidegger's analysis of Dasein brings the ontological disclosedness of Being in an original way.

Heidegger writes, "Dasein's facticity is such that it's Being-in-the-world has always dispersed itself or even split itself up into definite ways of Being-in. The multiplicity of these is indicated by the following examples; having to do with something, producing something, attending to something and looking after it, making use of something, giving something up and letting it go, undertaking, accomplishing, evincing, interrogating, considering, discussing, determining. All these ways of Being-in have concern.[49]

Being ontically asserts its existence in its concern for things, and for the worldhood of the world, manifest in practices such as environmentality, and equipmentality. Dasein is always preoccupied with resources, which it must use, discard, replenish, look for, eat, drink, etc. These practices are shared by Dasein in the forms of concern, care, mood, and fear. These practices are ways of being in the world with the they and are manifestations of everydayness.[50] These concerns are further crystalized in everydayness as idle talk, curiosity, ambiguity, throwness and falleness. These are ontic practices, but they are impregnated with ontological meanings, which Heidegger seeks to disclose. At this level, Heidegger is describing the metaphysics of the present embodied in everydayness, as the activities of the they.

Dasein, as Being, is manifested as care, mood, and anxiety. Anxiety and dread are temporal features of Dasein, as well. One of Dasein's utmost concerns is the fear of death as a projection of Dasein's existential projection and grounds for despair and dread, as it moves toward death in the form of sickness—Kierkegaard was the first to capture this form of fear. The fear, when understood ontologically, is unnecessary, since death itself is a phenomenon of life, and that life, ontologically, is a steady movement toward death, as the end of an ontic reality, but, the beginning of ontological possibility, a potential description of the not-yet. The not-yet is one of the forms that Dasein makes its very own, a move toward the future and away from the dead past and moody present.

As Heidegger put it, "Let the term 'dying' stand for that way of Being in which Dasein is towards death. Accordingly, we must say that Dasein never perishes. Dasein, however, can demise only as long as it is dying. . . . The existential Interpretation of death takes precedence over any biology and ontology of life."[51]

Existence, facticity, and falling are modes of Being in the world with the anxious they, when Dasein is there. Dying itself, as demise, is grounded in care. Being is concerned, afraid, anxious, and anguished about dying. This anxiety, however, is existentially misplaced, once we understand the meaning of Being ontologically, as a movement toward death. We can doubt the present, as Descartes does in the *First Meditation*, (summarized above), but we cannot doubt death. We *are* because we are fated to die. It is that fact that Dasein is absolutely sure of. Dying is a fact that we cannot doubt. Reason can doubt everything, but it cannot doubt the fact that the human knows with absolute certainty that we shall die. Death is the destiny of Dasein. The they are meant to die, it is this inevitability that becomes sickness unto death.

Dasein itself is "an impassioned freedom towards death."[52] An ontological analysis of Being releases the inner structure of Being toward death and frees Dasein from the idle talk of the they, toward the sunlight of freedom, expunging sickness unto death, as Kierkegaard, before Heidegger, put it.

Once this ontological status of life as a movement toward death is given, Being begins to realize its future possibilities and potentiated existence in time and history. Death itself is part of the flow, and "Dasein can resolutely come to terms with the inevitability of death, in distinction to dying, resolutely," in which Dasein hands itself down to itself, free from death, in a possibility which it has inherited, and yet has chosen.[53]

Dasein understands that it is part of the inherited past and the not-yet future, that it is rooted in history factually but can also project into the future, and that ways of existence in the forms of race, sex, and gender belong to the realm of the not-yet—although we begin by accepting their presentness in the norms and practices of the they.

As Heidegger puts it most eloquently, "Only an entity which in its Being, is essentially Futural so that it is free for its death and can let itself be thrown back upon its factical "there" by shattering itself against death—that is to say, only an entity which, as futural, is equipprimordially in the process of having been, can, by handing down to itself the possibility it has inherited, take over its own throwness and be in the moment of vision for 'it's time'. Only authentic temporality which is at the same time finite, makes possible something like fate—that is to say, authentic historicality."[54]

Race, sex, and gender, in this reading are factical inheritance but can be transcended temporally and historically by authentic resoluteness. Facing one's death requires a mastery of fear and anxiety to prepare oneself to exit from the factical world of the they toward the open future, the zone of possibilities, the not-yet, the horizon of natality.

Heidegger returns to these themes, most powerfully in *Discourse on Thinking*. In that work of his mature years, the theme of self-mastery as a path toward the founding of the metaphysics of Being is analyzed through the nature of thinking. It is only when we think about what we are doing, that we will consciously fashion a Self with new ethics and aesthetics of existence. In that small but potent book, Heidegger provokes us to think while doing and to think about what we are doing. The whatness of existence is revisited through *Meditative Thinking*, a radical form of thinking that releases us toward worldhood, but this time, the world as our very own, the world in which we are not merely present because we are born there, but a world that we renew anew with every act of thinking. This releasement, as Heidegger calls it, is a movement, a path, which Dasein must embark on. Although this is a long stretch, this movement is a kind of becoming, a construction of our bodies and genders, thoughtfully and meaningfully.

As the teacher put it, "Because that-which-regions regions all, gathering everything together and letting everything return to itself, to rest to its own identity"[55]

That identity could easily take self-fashioned sexual orientations and gender identities, is an outcome of Dasein futural, as Heidegger would say.

I must now turn attention to the Simone de Beauvoir's feminist discourse as a text on modernity and the sexed and gendered subject.

B. SIMONE DE BEAUVOIR

For Simone de Beauvoir, women, in particular, choose sex and gender in situations of historical domination perpetuated my men. Sex and gender are in fact outcomes of choice. They are not permanently fixed categories of nature, and that anatomy is not destiny.

For her, women are born in violence. Two powerful passages make this point, "Woman? Very simple, say the fanciers of simple formulas: she is a womb, an ovary; she is female."[56]

"Even when she is willing, or proactive, it is unquestionably the male who takes the female—she is taken . . . the male seizes her and holds her in place; he performs the copulatory movements; and among insects, birds, and mammals, he penetrates her. In that penetration her inwardness is violated, she is an enclosure that is broken into."[57]

The male penetrates her, and that penetration marks her for life—as something could be entered into—whether she likes it or not. Penetration is a symbol of violence. It is an imposition of the male on the female, even when done gently. Therefore, woman is born through violence. Her biology is used against her. Her inner dignity is violated. Her interior is turned inside out, not merely metaphorically. Her resistance to violence is the source of man's pleasure. She is reduced to a thing, and the man emerges as the victor, the founding conqueror of the woman's condition, the one who put the woman in her "place." She did not choose this condition. The limitations of her physicality are the grounds of the humiliation. The success of the penetrator is the ultimate justification of his manhood, his superiority. Thus is established the first rule of civilization, the woman must be put in her place. She has to know where she can appear and where she cannot, and how she must appear, on man's terms. She is not asked. She is acted upon. The man is actional. The woman is servile, with a submissive style and patience. She must smile, look happy, and appear effeminate, delicate, and voiceless. Voice is male. Listening is female.

This is how civilization began as a relation between two biological frames, man and woman—the passage from the state of nature to the state of culture.

There is a psychoanalytic move also, in which the woman is framed as a mutilated man, a frustrated being with an Electra complex, which pushes her to desire her father. Contrary to Freud, she admires the independence and individuality of her father, but does not necessarily desire her father, as in the Oedipal complex, in which the boy sexually desires his mother. Sadly, contends de Beauvoir, "On the other hand, the concept of the Electra Complex is very vague, because, it is not supported by a basic description of the feminine libido."[58] As in the biological frame, this too is modeled on a masculine Freudian reading of a complex reality. In both instances the woman is defined by a masculine linguistic construct and symbolic assumptions. In both situations, woman is reduced to her body. She is not allowed to live her body; rather her body is defined by the man so that she can live in it as she is supposed to, according to the biological facts and psychoanalytical premises that define what a woman is. Woman is defined by man and not permitted the choice to define herself. The biological data of woman has already defined her, and she is expected to live out that definition, only. de Beauvoir argues, "The true problem for a woman is to reject these flights from reality and seek self-fulfillment in transcendence."[59] As Heidegger and Sartre would have said, and from whom de Beauvoir draws, woman is not merely facticity, but also transcendence, not only a body, but also a possibility, a freedom. These visions of being a woman are lost on both the biologists and the psychoanalysts.

When the woman asserts herself, she is not merely being virile, male, that is but herself, expressing and living what she feels in spite of her body, her facticity. She asserts herself as a human being who happens to be a woman, and not a woman who is attempting to be a man. She is not an imitative woman, but a woman who is transcending her imposed situation.[60]

de Beauvoir concludes, "I conceive her as hesitating between the role of object, Other, which is offered her, and the assertion of her liberty."[61] Furthermore, "The value of muscular strength, of the phallus, of the tool can be defined only, in a world of values; it is determined, by the basic project through which the existent seeks transcendence."[62] Her point is that if there are physical differences between men and women, the tasks that we assign to them, and the weight of the values that are attached to those tasks, are determined by men in power. If we change the values then the physical differences do not determine destiny, they are arbitrary and discriminatory devices that we use to justify oppression. The situation of women is determined by these tools of power.

de Beauvoir proceeds to test these propositions through some historical lenses and learns that primitive societies, as she calls them, had similar visions of women. Woman as a creator of life was looked at with high regard in contrast to man, the physically strong killer. Killing was valued more highly than creating, and "Here we have the key to the whole mystery."[63]

Even in matrilineal societies, where women held leadership positions, women were not sovereign enough to affect the conditions of the poor, as in the case of Catherine the Great, who did not do enough to change the miserable conditions of peasant women.[64]

Ancient peoples subjected women to being pleasure givers to guests and made women prostitutes, as in fifth century Babylon where women were duty bound to yield themselves to strangers "in the temple of Mylitta for Money."[65] Similarly, among the Greeks and the Orientals, the rich and powerful were allowed to have three to four wives, whereas the peasants rarely were allowed more than two. Wives were also valued relative to their wealth. The richer they were, the greater their dignity, except for in ancient Egypt where there was no private property.[66]

Nor did the French Revolution change much, as women remained in a subordinate position. In the eyes of philosophers like Rousseau, or writers such as Balzac, the function of women was to provide pleasure to men. They were not considered full persons, but subordinates to men, exactly as in ancient societies. Women were exploited sexually and economically, underpaid when employed, or simply kept at home to create and not be respected for it.[67]

Moreover, women are also objects of myths which articulate the fantasies, fears, and dreams of men. God is thanked for giving woman to man. She is an object that can be given and taken away at man's will. Her situation is that of an Other, without sovereignty. Woman is at once an idol, a servant, a slave, a magician, gossip, falsehood, source of truth, healing presence, sorceress, man's prey, downfall, strange, complicated, and confused, as Kierkegaard described her. She is everything that man is not. She is an Other, a mythical Other.[68]

Writers have also mythologized woman. Montherlant looks at her as solar spirit and seeks animality in her; Lawrence, demands the feminine sex from her; she is a soul sister to Claudel; Breton roots woman in nature; Stendhal wants her as an intelligent mistress and as an equal. These are not qualities the woman chooses for herself under conditions of freedom. These are man's demands, the meaning of woman being imposed on her.[69] Note that in all these dreams about her, the woman is not addressed as someone who has a view, a vision of herself. No. Categorically No. She is the Other, who lives for the man, to live his dreams, his fantasies, his fears, and his anguish. She is surely an existent, who lives in a man's world. In that world, she is not a movement toward death, like all beings, but a passive consummation of man's possibilities. Man is a subject, who acts resolutely. Woman is an object, who cannot live her life completely. She is Dasein. She has no agency.

de Beauvoir begins to trace the woman's world, and therein begins with childhood. As a child, the woman again lives not in her body by determining its needs, but as a reaction to the man's whims. Her life begins as that of a doll, who must ornament herself and make herself beautiful for the man. The man's world responds by calling her pretty or homely. She becomes the subject of aesthetic complements, impregnated with sexual interest. In this way she objectifies herself, by making herself a thing. She learns early on that she must make herself beloved to the man, and by so doing she awaits love. The man is the subject, the movement who moves toward her, and she, she is the object who must be moved on. There is no equality in this situation.

In this environment, woman is a Cinderella, a Sleeping Beauty, a Snow White. She is always receiving and endlessly submitting to make it in a man's world. Soon enough, the young girl wakes up to the fact that she must renounce her independence and hide her intelligence and dreams in a man's world in order to succeed at capturing a husband. Submission becomes her new way of life. The man likes it that way. He is action. He must initiate, and the woman responds. Her mother early on advises her to do so, because the mother, who was once the little girl, knows so.[70] The mother counsels her to be a woman, in a man's world.

The young girl is now groomed to be a woman. She is introduced to sexuality on her way to marriage, full of complexities and ambiguities, described in detail, and leading to the choice of lesbianism, when young girls are unsatisfied by man's domination of the sexual act.[71]

de Beauvoir writes, "Homosexuality is no more a perversion deliberately indulged in than it is a curse of fate. It is an attitude chosen in a certain situation—that is, at once motivated and freely adopted. Like all human behavior, homosexuality leads to make believe, disequilibrium, frustration, lies, or, on the contrary becomes the source of rewarding experiences, in accordance with its manner of expression in actual living—whether in bad faith, laziness, and falsity, or in lucidity, generosity and freedom."[72]

Motherhood gives women an extraordinary sense of Self, in that they are creating humans, raising them, cultivating them, and teaching them language, manners, morals. Women are not only housewives, sex machines, care givers, in short, objects who live for others. No. Women in fact are the builders of civilization, the voices of conscience, and mediators of consciousness. Motherhood gives the woman subjectivity, individuality, and a creative power superior to that of a man. Motherhood brings out worldhood and means concretely being in the world. It is Dasein actuated.[73]

Woman is not always a victim. As just noted, she is the moral educator of the muscle-bound man's civilization. The narcissist woman and the woman in love are leaders of women's liberty. The narcissist woman, who does not need the man's gaze, looks at herself in the mirror and realizes her physicality, her self-admired beauty.. She gazes at herself and judges herself by internally generated standards of beauty. As one woman put it, "I am adorable, I am simply adorable. . . Another woman said, "I love myself, I am my God."[74] de Beauvoir writes, "Despite her superficial arrogance, the narcissist realizes her precarious position; and this explains why she is uneasy, oversensitive, irritable, constantly on the watch; her vanity in insatiable. The older she grows, the more eagerly she seeks praise and success and the more suspicious she is of conspiracies around her; distracted, obsessed, she hides in the darkness of insincerity and often ends by forming around her a shell of delirious paranoia. There is a saying that is singularly appropriate in her case: "He that findeth his life shall lose it."[75]

The woman in love is different. She loses herself in her lover. She becomes him by making him, and everything he loves, her own. Her existence dissolves in his. She is not obsessed with herself as the narcissist woman is, but with her lover. She loves to wash his clothes, breathe his very air, read the books he loves. She makes herself love what he loves. She abandons her world, her dreams, in exchange for his. She lives in his world and helps the lover to realize his dreams. They become one, as she wants it, as when they simultaneously say, "we are pregnant." She becomes her lover's double. She wills the domination and willfully makes herself an object. The necessary condition for this situation is that she feels that her lover loves her, really.

All this changes when she feels unloved. de Beauvoir writes, "Genuine love ought to be founded on the mutual recognition of two liberties; the lovers would then experience themselves both as self and as other: neither would give up transcendence, neither would be mutilated; together they would manifest values and aims in the world. For the one and the other. Love would be revelation of self by the gift of self and enrichment of the world."[76]

Such is the dream of the independent woman. Unlike the woman in love, the independent woman wishes to live in her body; own the streets on which she walks, without the annoying male gaze; she wants to carry the weight of the world on her shoulders, like great men do; she wants to own her universe as her intimate own by rejoicing in the good and correcting the excesses of progress. The independent woman, like geniuses of all time, desires to "enact the fate of all humanity in their personal existences, and no woman has believed herself authorized to do so."[77]

Such are the dreams of the independent woman—a self-defining political and moral subject—as presented by Simone de Beauvoir, the voice of self-constructing women for the future of humanity, when she concludes with a brilliant passage, "To emancipate woman is to refuse to confine her to the relations she bears to man, not to deny them to her; let her have her independent existence and she will continue none the less to exist for him also; mutually recognizing each other as subject, each will remain for the other another. The reciprocity of their relations will not do away with the miracles—desire, possession, love, dream, adventure worked by the division of human beings . . . on the contrary, when we abolish the slavery of half of humanity, together with the whole system of hypocrisy that it implies, then the division of humanity will reveal its genuine significance and the human couple will find its true form."[78]

C. FOUCAULT

Foucault, like de Beauvoir, wants to provide a genealogy and archeology of the binaries, man/woman, and also other possibilities, in the form of the history of sexuality. The history of sexuality since the seventeenth century is the history of repression, "after years of open spaces and free expression."[79]

Foucault opposes this hypothesis with the argument that there have been instances of freedom in the form of the deployment of sexuality, of dissemination, of polymorphous sexualities. In the first volume of *The History of Sexuality*, Foucault examines the history of these instances, which counter the repressive hypotheses, as Foucault calls it. For Foucault, "Western man has been drawn for three centuries to the task of telling everything concerning his sex."[80] Contrary to being repressed, sex has been deployed, analyzed, classified, and specified carefully. Moderns talk about sex more than they do about anything else. Sex is in everybody's mind. Repression has given way to dissemination. Curiosity is replaced by analysis and exposition of sex and more sex. The pornography industry has killed love and replaced it with sex, more and more sex. Magazines, books, movies, and television are selling sex by the second, and people are consuming these products. They salivate for these images that are being sold to them. Repression is displaced by deployment; openness about our interior lives is now the norm.

However, the dissemination came at a cost. Sex becomes classified as normal, abnormal, perverse. Sex becomes problematized. The possibilities of the self are evaluated, judged, and classified. Foucault writes, "From childhood to old age, a norm of sexual deployment was defined, and all the possible deviations were carefully described; pedagogical controls and medical treatments were organized; around the least fantasies, moralists, but especially doctors."[81]

Modernity has thus initiated sexual heterogeneities. They were deployed, not because sex had become lax, but rather that the deployment facilitates close supervision of deviant sexualities, so that experts could medicalize them and treat them as diseases. It is the deployment that makes it easier for the police of morality to study deviations close up, with minute scrutiny, and then filter through what is available in the market and evaluate the products by sifting through the normal and the pathological. More importantly, surveillance of sex now becomes the new norm of science and the medical profession and all the networks of the panopticon.

The homosexual now comes to the daylight to be studied and treated as a patient. Power is exercised as that which studies, questions, monitors, watches, spies, searches out, palpates, brings to light: capture and seduction, confrontation and mutual enforcement, parents and children, adults and adolescents, educator and students, doctors and patients, the psychiatrist with his hysteric and his perverts, all have played this game continually since the nineteenth century.

Repression gives way to the birth of the science of sexuality. The binaries are now the subjects of science. The state employs experts to identify the deviants, the bastards, and promises the citizens that it will free them from these deviations and eradicate perversions. The homosexual is now the enemy of the state. As Foucault puts it, "Western man has become a confessional animal."[82] A society of confessing animals comes into being, and a singular regime of truth becomes a way of life. Ars Erotica is displaced by Scientia Sexualis. Bodies and pleasures, the possibilities of the self are now medicalized as the subjects of science and the regimes of truth, which must be uncovered, unless abnormality is to ascend to power, and the fascist state intervenes to see to it that this does not happen.

The enjoyment of bodies and pleasure, as opposed to the science of bodies and pleasure, which are future possibilities of the self, particularly for homosexuals, is the subject of *The Use of Pleasure: The History of Sexuality, Volume Two*.

Following Plato in the *Symposium*, Foucault argues that the Greeks had a rather lax attitude toward homosexuality, like that of the pleasures of the self. True love could take the form of the love of boys. Following Plato, Foucault reports that, "love should be directed to the soul of boys rather than to their bodies."[83] In this way, argues Foucault, the concern with self-examination becomes a necessary condition for guiding the desire for young boys, as pleasure, as the search for truth, a search for self-imposed monitoring of oneself.[84] In the monitoring of self-required vigilance toward diet and health, as guided by an ethical standard of moderation, pleasure and truth become seamlessly combined, as practices of the self. Yet, concludes Foucault, "So that what was now at the core of the problematizing of sexual conduct was no longer pleasure, and the aesthetics of its use, but desire and its purifying hermeneutics."[85]

Of course, Foucault thinks that when the love of boys and men takes this ethical term, it can become a powerful way of life, an ethics of existence, and an example of self-fashioning, an aesthetic. This possibility was not available to the Greek imagination or the late Greek and Roman civilizations that followed. This alternative deployment of sexuality had to wait for Foucault, and later, Judith Butler, to imagine and work out, to the limits of modernity, to which I now turn.

D. JUDITH BUTLER

Judith Butler has openly declared her indebtedness to Simone de Beauvoir and Michel Foucault for the origin and development of queer theory and third-wave feminism. She is the voice of these possibilities of the Self, as developed in her classic work, *Gender Trouble*.

Her thesis is that sex and gender are both human constructions and that there is no such thing as a woman, a fixed appearance, even in a biological form. There is only a human form, which is later linguistically fixed as a woman, which is subsequently gendered as female. The move is arbitrary, but also politically charged, in that it pathologizes human yearnings that are not part of the "normal" linguistic idiom. The fixed representation of the form as a woman is later manipulated by the networks of the State and then diffused to society at large, where the unstable category of woman is repeatedly performed and then internalized as a way of life. Woman, as we learned from Simone de Beauvoir, is a performance, and not an essence. For Butler, woman is nothing more than a repeated practice, a doing, a preforming, as opposed to being. That is what Butler means by woman is performativity. Being a female for Butler is not a natural fact either. It is a culturally performed habit. Both sex and the gender that follows are performative acts of imposition on the self, most particularly the unaware self. For the vigilant persons who would like to choose for themselves, varying sexual orientations are resisted by informed political action in the form of feminist movements.

Because of this confusion, feminists themselves have assumed that there is something called a woman, which all women share, whose rights and liberties must be defended by the law, or juridical fiat. If there is no woman, or female, that represents all women and females, there are no rights and liberties to defend. In Butler's own words, "The very subject of women is no longer understood in stable or abiding terms. There is a great deal of material that not only questions the viability of "the subject" as the ultimate candidate for representation or, indeed, liberation, but there is very little agreement after all on what it is that constitutes, or ought to constitute, the category of women."[86] In others words, before women can be represented as bearers of rights or possessors of freedom, it must be understood what the form of woman is. What is a woman after all?—is a question that merits analysis. The term woman itself must be freed from the trap of heterosexual normativity of imposed definition.

Butler challenges feminists to rethink the question of woman and female before they proceed to represent her universally. The political assumption that womanhood has a universal basis must be questioned with critique in the Foucauldian sense of questioning the presence of the present, or, the metaphysics of the present.

Butler agrees with de Beauvoir in that "the female body ought to be the situation and instrumentality of women's freedom, and not a defining and limiting essence."[87]

Furthermore, the female body is heterosexualized by being given a stable and definite identity that women themselves did not choose. Women find themselves living the heterosexual situation framed by masculinity, when it contrasts itself from femininity, and imposes the latter on women. The woman is first sexed, and then suitably gendered. Her gender is a logical consequence of her sex. These are syllogistically conceptualized definitions of women by the masculinist language of heterosexuality.[88] Again, even the syllogistic arguments are themselves deliberately articulated by men to prevent women to counter these syllogisms, and too smoothly refined to be taken seriously. Women must perform their own syllogisms that address their needs and self-definitions.

Furthermore, Butler notes, "Rubin further maintains that before the transformation of a biological male or female into a gendered man or woman, 'each child contains all of the sexual possibilities available to human expression.'"[89]

In short, for Butler, there is no biological male or female. There are only anatomical possibilities without culturally fixed names. As she puts it, "That penis, vagina, breasts and so forth, are named sexual parts is both a restriction of the erogenous body to those parts and a fragmentation of the body as a whole."[90] If the self is empowered to employ its imagination freely, it might as well reconfigure the function of the sexual parts. Sexuality need not be restricted just to those two parts. The other parts of the body are also sources of sexual pleasure. That the "unity" and "integrity" of the body is the effect of power, as Foucault concluded, and which Butler reinforces approvingly. As she puts it, "For Foucault, the body is not "sexed" in any significant sense . . . The body gains meaning within discourse only in the context of power relations . . . as such, Sexuality as understood by Foucault, is to produce sex as an artificial concept which effectively extends and disguises the power relations responsible for its genesis."[91] In short, power first produces sexuality, reduces it to sex, and then moves on to culture, producing gender, and then reduces sex to gender and gender to sex. Both linguistic designations are products of power, including the biology of the Self; a neutral biology is reduced to sex first and gender later. These identities of the Self are significations imposed by power, and endlessly performed, until they become firmly entrenched habits. Woman, female, man, and male are effects of power imposed by the masculine gaze masquerading as the natural order of the world, when they are actually cultural constructions.

Butler speaks for herself, when she concludes, "I have tried to suggest that the identity categories often presumed to be foundational to feminist politics, that is, deemed necessary in order to mobilize feminism as an identity politics, simultaneously work to limit and constrain in advance the very cultural possibilities that feminism is supposed to open up. The tacit constraints that produce culturally intelligible "sex" ought to be understood as generative political structures rather than naturalized foundations. Paradoxically, the reconceptualization of identity as an effect, that is, as produced or generated, opens up possibilities of "agency" that are insidiously foreclosed . . . as foundational and fixed."[92] In my terms, this idea, which Butler suggests, opens up a new horizon of self-definitions for the oppressed self. I will return to this theme in the last chapter on self-definition, where I will articulate my own vision of definitions for the Self.

NOTES

49. Martin Heidegger, *Being and Time*, translated by John McQuarrie and Edward Robinson (New York: Harper & Row, 1962), 83.
50. Ibid., 83–219.
51. Ibid., 291.
52. Ibid., 311.
53. Ibid., 435.
54. Ibid., 437.
55. Martin Heidegger, *Discourse on Thinking* (New York: Harper & Row, 1966), 86.
56. Simone De Beauvoir, *The Second Sex* (New York: Vintage Books, 1989), 3.
57. Ibid., 21.
58. Ibid., 22.
59. Ibid., 51.
60. Ibid., 51.

61. Ibid., 52.
62. Ibid., 60.
63. Ibid., 64.
64. Ibid., 71–72.
65. Ibid., 89.
66. Ibid., 88.
67. Ibid., 109–38.
68. Ibid., 143.
69. Ibid., 251.
70. Ibid., 328–89.
71. Ibid., 371–404.
72. Ibid., 424.
73. Ibid., 487–526.
74. Ibid., 632.
75. Ibid., 641.
76. Ibid., 667.
77. Ibid., 713.
78. Ibid., 731.
79. Michel Foucault, *The History of Sexuality: Volume 1: An Introduction* (New York: Vintage Books, 1980), 5.
80. Ibid., 23.
81. Ibid., 36.
82. Ibid., 59.
83. Michel Foucault, *The Use of Pleasure: Volume Two* (New York: Vintage Books, 1985), 238.
84. Ibid., 250.
85. Ibid., 254.
86. Judith Butler, *Gender Trouble: Feminism and the Subversion of Identity* (New York: Routledge, 1990), 1.
87. Ibid., 12.
88. Ibid., 22–23.
89. Ibid., 73–74.
90. Ibid., 114.
91. Ibid., 92.
92. Ibid., 147.

· *10* ·

Revolutionary Theory and Race

*I*n this chapter I critically examine the idea of race and how it is deployed in the lives of the black self, humans who are born with a black skin, in a world that oppresses them.

A. PHILOSOPHICAL REREADING OF FANON, NKRUMAH, AND CABRAL IN THE AGE OF GLOBALIZATION AND POST-MODERNITY

I will examine three themes to which Frantz Fanon, Kwame Nkrumah, and Amilcar Cabral devoted lifelong reflections. I will address these themes in three parts:

   I. Fanon and the African/Black Self
  II. Nkrumah and the African Personality
 III. Cabral and Returning to the Origins of the African Self and the Construction of an Autonomous African Socialist Path

Part I: Fanon and the African/Black Self

The nature and historical ordeals of the black self are first articulated in Fanon's foundational 1952 text, *Black Skin, White Masks*. In that book, Fanon asks what it means to be black. He answers, "The black man has two dimensions. One with his fellows and the other with the white man. . . . That this self-division is a direct result of colonialist subjugation is beyond question."[93] Fanon is careful to emphasize, as Lewis Gordon, one of his premier interpreters points out,[94] that his characterization does not apply to all blacks and whites. As Fanon put it in the introduction to *Black Skin, White Masks*, "Many Negroes will not find themselves in what follows. This is equally true of many whites."[95] The analysis focuses on unhealthy blacks and unhealthy whites, products of colonial subjugation. This crucial point is often overlooked in Fanon studies, leading to misreading.

In his detailed psycho-existential and phenomenological analysis of the alienated black Self, Fanon is wisely conscious that there are many healthy blacks and whites that do not fit the description, and once the analysis is performed, the distorted reality that it depicts will be destroyed by political action, led by the African self—as occurs in Fanon's last, world famous book, *The Wretched of the Earth* (1961).

The alienated black is an other to himself/herself. He/she is neither black nor white. The alienated black has no identity except for the peculiar kind of blackness that is imposed by the white man. The alienated black is a construction of white colonization. That identity is niggerization. The black is now a nigger, a non-being. The black person is now simply called a nigger, "Dirty Nigger," or, said simply, "Look, a Negro."[96]

Of course, Fanon, the conscious analyst of this distorted condition, immediately notes, "'Look, a Negro!' It was true. It amused me . . . but I rejected all immunization of the emotions. I wanted to be a man, nothing but a man."[97]

Fanon, the medical doctor, is contending that the black came to this world to be celebrated and accepted like any other human being, to be a human being. The black does exactly that to tragically discover that alienated whites do not recognize her as a human being like any other, but rather as a black non-human, an object among other objects, like chairs and tables, without an ontological status. The medical doctor here is observing the black condition as a narrator who knows who he is. Fanon, the critic, is diagnosing the unhealthy black and white condition.

It is as if Fanon, the proud black doctor, wants to answer back and say, Look, a handsome black man with a rich global history. Indeed, that is exactly what he must have said in his heart, the organ of living thought. But that is another matter.

"The black that is now simply a nigger is scripted and narrated by the white man. The white man knows the black as a nigger. The black is fixed by language and is in language. The black is constructed by the white gaze—the look, which knows the nigger, as if the black person is "a chemical solution . . . fixed by a dye."[98] The black as a nigger is a non-being, without an ontology. Where there is no being, there is no ontology. The nigger in the zone of non-being a "sterile and arid region,"[99] is without ontology, without a human structure.

In order for the black person to have an ontology two conditions must be present: (1) that there is a human being whose structure can be described, (2) that there are customs and traditions that affirm the black's existence. The colonizers systematically destroyed both conditions. In this way, the black person's being was erased. The erasure was conducted in order to argue that the black person is not fully human. Therefore, the black person is inferior to the white person, and ontology does not apply to the black. The black therefore, is simply a nigger, without being and without history.

Fanon, the critic, is insisting that the alienated black is not merely a nigger but a human being. The black person now discovers that his/her ancestors are founders of world civilizations; that they originated philosophy, astronomy, mathematics; were the teachers of Thales, Pythagoras, Plato, Aristotle, and many more; and that they carved pyramids, obelisks, and churches out of stone in Egypt and Ethiopia.[100] Also, the black person now knows there are alienated blacks who deny their blackness. Fanon, the critic, is not one of them. He describes the alienated black condition in order to destroy it through practice. Analysis must precede action. Diagnosis leads to prognoses. Fanon, the medical doctor, has diagnosed the black condition in its niggerized and alienated form. The rehabilitation of the alienated Negro requires an objective diagnosis of her condition.

The Global south is a source of values of all kinds and not merely the house of niggers who are good for nothing, and who must be kept in their place, by force if necessary. As Fanon puts it, "I feel in myself a soul as immense as the world, truly a soul as deep as the deepest of rivers, my chest has the power to expand without limit . . . without responsibility, straddling Nothingness and Infinity, I began to weep."[101]

Weeping is cathartic. Weeping is a revolutionary release of repressed anger. It paves the road toward freedom, toward the tranquilly of truth. The truth is that "the black" is not merely a sexual machine, a criminal, a biological danger, but a human being who was colonized, exploited, lynched, enslaved, and despised by a capitalist society, denuded of his ontology and buried in the zone of non-being.[102] These facts are documented in the brilliant pages of *Black Skin, White Masks*.

The prognoses for the diagnostics of *Black Skin, White Masks* is now offered in *The Wretched of the Earth*. These two texts are intimately connected. In *Black Skin, White Masks*, Fanon is already pointing toward *The Wretched of the Earth*, when he notes that the black must be actional (proactive) to change the alienated black condition.[103] Actionality is the necessary and sufficient condition for overcoming the paralysis of blackness in the black world that *Black Skin, White Masks* presents.

I dub *The Wretched of the Earth* the philosophical and political construct of the actional imaginary. In *The Wretched of the Earth* the black person speaks and acts as an African. The black is now an African Self.

The Wretched of the Earth begins with a call for actionality, when Fanon writes, "Decolonization is a violent phenomenon . . . it is a program of complete disorder."[104] These powerful words have not always been understood calmly. Many have used this observation to portray Fanon as the apostle of violence. And yet Fanon is not cavalierly instructing the African person to take up arms and butcher the colonizers. Fanon does not advocate violence anywhere. Rather, the argument must first be put analytically.

X is Y
Therefore,
B is also Y.

X is Colonialism
Y is violent
B is decolonization
Y is violent

In other words, for Fanon, the violence in the colonial relationship is "built in"; therefore, it cannot be a matter of advocating it. The relationship between colonization and decolonization is fated to take the tragic form of counter violence in the new form of revolutionary violence. It is in this sense that colonization, which gave us the black as a nigger, by using guns, bayonets, books, and religion to distort the personality of the black, can be overhauled in the same way it came, through violence. The black that has discovered her Africanity and affirms this new African Self by actionality must now dissolve the structures of violence, which produced the alienated black condition. Revolutionary violence must normalize the abnormality of the colonial condition and the equally abnormal blacks and whites, which it has produced.

Violence as action frees the alienated black who was forced to hate herself. Fanon contends, "At the level of individuals, violence is a cleansing force."[105] It empowers the African native to celebrate her history, her language, her customs and traditions, the necessary and sufficient condition of articulating the black ontology as diagnosed in *Black Skin, White Masks*.

The African self now learns that the white person is just another human, neither inferior nor superior but a violator of the right of the African. Colonialism was the organized form of this violation. This violation of African rights must now be combated by action, by giving one's life to restore the stolen African legacy. The African now knows that the white man can be defeated and that decolonization must happen.[106] Violence humbles the white colonizer, who thinks and lives like he is a member of a superior race. Once the colonized blacks defeat him, the colonized blacks will be empowered to confront the colonizers and realize the process of decolonization, at the rendezvous with revolutionary history. In the end, violence cleanses both the colonizer and the colonized, of hate, of the superiority, and inferiority complexes.

Decolonization, however, is not fully supported by the African intellectual. The African intellectual is an opportunist, whereas the African masses have nothing to lose if they give their total commitment to the decolonizing project. For the African masses, the struggle to free themselves from the brutalities of colonization is a moral and political imperative. For the African intellectuals it is an opportunity, which they can afford to miss if the colonizers buy them through money and ranks.

At this point decolonization enters a new phase of creating tension between the exploited masses who want to fight the colonizers to the bitter end and alienated African intellectuals who seek to put a brake on the continental struggles.

The masses have nothing to lose from continuing the fight, whereas the shortsighted opportunist intellectuals want to sit in cushy positions and look at the shantytowns of globalization. Contemporary Globalization is propelled by the silence of pseudo-African leaders, sucking the leftovers of neo-colonialism.

The intellectuals founded non-inclusive political parties; they ignore the backbone of decolonization, namely the peasantry of the countryside, who in turn fundamentally mistrust the party leaders. The political parties, along with the unions who organize the workers of the city, do not trust one another. As Fanon put it, "The Unions, the parties, or the government in a kind of immortal Machiavellian fashion all make use of the peasant masses as a blind, inert tactical force: brute force, as it were."[107]

Fanon was an acute observer of spontaneous violence unrestrained by political reason. He warned against the dangers of the spontaneity of the angry African masses.

Fanon, the philosopher of actionality, advises that the peasantry, along with the lumpenproletariat of the shantytowns, must now be restrained. Spontaneous violence and brute force must now be controlled. The decolonial project led by the political parties must be rethought and actionality must be organized. His experience in the Algerian FLN taught him a lesson first hand: that spontaneity is only a sufficient condition for the earlier phases of decolonization and that a mature decolonization under the leadership of a genuine political party must organize the peasantry of the countryside, the workers of the cities, and the lumpenproletariat. Algeria is the focus of this anatomy of dying colonialism.[108]

Fanon is now a theorist of revolutionary violence. For Fanon, disorganized spontaneity leads to blind nationalism without a purpose. Genuine nationalism must be organized by a national consciousness, and the two are not the same. Nationalism is organized by opportunistic intellectuals who founded nationalistic political parties without a vision of the Common Good of the African continent. By this time, Fanon has become a Pan-Africanist.

The new Africa requires new leaders. Organic leaders must replace the opportunistic leaders who exploit the spontaneity of the masses. The new leaders must be educators who organize spontaneity and replace it with a disciplined national consciousness. These new leaders, in the form of councils, must invite the participation of the people to imagine their future. The people's councils, the people's public fora, must displace political parties.

Fanon invites the people to directly participate in deciding the needs of the African continent. Actionality is now rooted in direct democracy.[109] The people represent themselves, directly. The pitfalls of nationalism can be avoided only if the people organize themselves and plan for their nations, collectively.[110]

Fanon writes, "No leader, however, valuable he may be, can substitute himself for the popular will; and the national government, before concerning itself about international prestige, ought first to give their dignity to all citizens, fill their minds and feast their eyes with human things, and create a prospect that is human because conscious and sovereign men dwell therein."[111]

The self-hating nigger of *Black Skin, White Masks* is now a citizen conscious of his ontology and capable of articulating a vision for a continent proud of its national cultures. The bad habits of the colonial world are replaced by the customs and traditions of the peasantry. Life in the world of the peasantry is reinvigorated and embraced critically, but lovingly and respectfully.[112] The bad customs are rejected and the good customs and practices are valued and treated as potential sources of an African imaginary. Africa is now a source of universal values for the human species, a home for new human beings of the world. This theme was also analyzed painstakingly in his *Toward the African Revolution*, a collection of brilliant essays, which were published [posthumously] in 1964.

As Fanon put it, "This new humanity cannot do otherwise than define a new humanism both for itself and for others."[113]

Fanon is not an apostle of violence but an original globalist from the neglected south, who analyzed and helped destroy the process of niggerization and replace it with a new globalist radical humanism, anchored on direct democracy.

Part II: Kwame Nkrumah and the African Personality

Nkrumah begins his book *Consciencism* by examining the history of philosophy in three brilliant chapters, which provide a masterful understanding and judicious critique of the Western philosophical tradition. He writes, "The history of a nation is, unfortunately, too easily written as the history of its dominant class. But if the history of a nation, or a people, cannot be found in the history of a class, how much less can the history of a continent be found in what is not even a part of it—Europe. Africa cannot be validly treated merely as the space in which Europe swelled up."[114]

For Nkrumah, African liberation presupposes the existence of an African Self: knowledgeable and proud of African history and eager to document the achievements of African people everywhere, as part and parcel of global history. Critically conscious scholars of all nationalities must understand African history through an African lens. The historian must only be honest, critical, informed, and unprejudiced by his background, particularly if he is from the global north. The necessary and sufficient qualification for the task is a blend of intelligence, integrity, compassion, and a passion for truth.

In chapter four, Nkrumah enters the heart of his philosophical project, *Consciencism*, the very title of his book.

Personality is nothing more than a conscious moral organization of the human self. African personality, therefore, is a conscious moral organization of the African self as a historically traumatized self that withstood the savageries and barbarism of all those who enslaved and colonized Africans everywhere. The critically conscious African personality is guided by historical facts about the African past and is keenly aware of African possibilities, which grow out of the class struggles waged both among Africans and against the Imperial project of neo-colonialism, which Nkrumah designated as the last stage of capitalism.

The fundamental thesis of *Consciencism* is that the African self, and for that matter the human self, must be treated as an end, with dignity, and with certain inalienable rights. For Nkrumah, this vision of the self is the organizing principle of the humanist and socialist traditions.[115]

The African personality is a bearer of this principle. The African person's material and non-material needs must be satisfied unconditionally, since the African person comes out from matter, and matter itself has a spiritual grounding, a fact that applies equally to all human beings.

The African personality, however, must liquidate colonialism and imperialism in order to become the bearer of dignity and to become a human end, whose rights cannot be violated. Central to that project is the end of class struggles within Africa, which are linked with colonialism and imperialism.[116]

This possibility requires positive action. Like Fanon, Nkrumah views the African person as having agency and a capacity to change the human condition.[117]

The African Self, according to Nkrumah, draws from three powerful sources of ontology: Christianity, Islam, and African socialism. Christianity and Islam, as religions, are rooted in idealism; that is, they are ideas outside the realm of matter. African socialism draws from the materialism of Marxism. Nkrumah, as a disciplined philosopher, seeks to reconcile idealism and materialism, so that he can consistently argue that African socialism overcomes the dualisms of matter and ideas by making both reconcilable sources of the African personality.

Like Fanon before him and Cabral after him, Nkrumah sees the African personality as a new synthetic whole. The necessary and sufficient condition for this original synthesis is African unity. Nkrumah's foundational premise is that in order for this synthesis to occur, a united Africa must collectively overthrow imperialism and colonialism. A united Africa requires a new revolutionary organizing principle—African personality is that organizing principle. The principle must provide Africa with a new economic vision, which is African Marxism, drawing from an African communitarian tradition, Christianity and Islam.

The African personality can come to being only after decolonization. Class rule in Africa must be systematically dismantled, and Africans must be freed from any form of exploitation. Socialism is precisely the new democratic form that fits the African personality.

The new humanity, which Fanon asked for in *The Wretched of the Earth*, can now be realized by the activities of the new African personality. The new African personality can give the world the much-needed compassion, the spirit of sharing, rich spirituality, and solidarity, which Fanon observed were characteristics of African communities. His point is not that African communities singularly own these values, but, more modestly, that these values, which were once part of humanity, have been destroyed by capitalism, whereas they have been preserved in pre-capitalist African value systems. Nkrumah calls for their reawakening and the possibility of constructing new world personalities. Central to this project is the dissolution of capitalism and imperialism, which ought to be the activity of workers and peasants working in unison by harmonizing their goals and defining an African common good out of African communitarianism, Islam, and Christianity, the three streams of African history.

Part III: Cabral, Returning to the Origins of the African Self, and the Construction of an Autonomous African Socialist Path

Cabral, a Lusophone thinker, closely follows Fanon and Nkrumah's vision that the African self must draw from the living sources of Africa's repressed national culture. Cabral argues that the African intellectual must return to this source, not to fossilize it, but to make it a dynamic fount of African development. For Cabral, culture is a force of progress and development. The African self must use the past to propel the present, to give the present motion and energy. The people's passions and imaginations can be mobilized by culture. Culture is the people's inner source of creativity and originality. Continental culture can serve as the people's source of actional imaginary and inspiration to engage in a global project of constructing new human beings, who are sincere, loving, intelligent, and passionate for truth.

Cabral reminds us that the people are fighting to better their lives by procuring the basic needs of the human being. Beyond that, the people hope decolonization can move their lives forward, that the future will be infinitely superior to the past. It is this vision, this dream of the possible, which draws them to join the struggle and fight for those who will come after them. The people are aware of their intergenerational obligations.

The people know that the future about which they dream can only come about when they resist the violation of their dignities and the contamination of their historic personalities. They also know that they must not let the retrogressive facets of culture hold them back. They must create new cultures of resistance, new modes of resisting the dead weight of the past, which they must combat with the new waves of popular culture created during the time of the struggle in association with the new people they meet. Together, they can construct original revolutionary personalities.[118]

For Cabral, culture is the most potent form of resistance to colonialism and imperialism. Once the people become aware that they have a national culture and an identity, they cannot be told that they have no ontology, as Fanon's nigger was forced to believe. Cabral was acutely aware of this Fanonian insight, which he used to organize the resistance in Cape Verde and Guinea Bissau.[119]

Furthermore, culture, argues Cabral, is a product of history. To the extent that a people have a culture, they are by definition a historical people. Culture is to history, Cabral notes, as a flower is to a plant. We cannot have one without the other. The victims of colonialism, then, must use culture to resist internal and external domination. For the people culture is a material force, which is also a productive force. In Marxian language, to which Cabral was devoted, culture belongs to both the base and the superstructure. Culture is simultaneously matter and idea. It influences both. A people with a culture is conscious of its material force and its ideational power.[120]

National liberation movements, in the end, are critically conscious organizers of culture as a material and non-material force in their resistance to colonial domination and in the articulation of the decolonial project of sustained resistance to colonialism, capitalism, and imperialism at the same time.

In the first stage of decolonization, popular culture, the cultures of all the varied classes—the rural dwellers, the urban dwellers and the privileged—must be mobilized. All these variants of culture are important in the resistance against cultural imperialism. As the struggle intensifies and matures, the various classes who interact begin to see the cultures as deeply connected. Together, they begin to develop new cultures out of their sustained interactions, suspicions give way to solidarity, and racial hostilities defer to human bonding. Racism is replaced by humanism. A new humanity begins to be born.[121]

All the facets of culture must be used in the struggle against colonialism and cultural imperialism. Even the members of the privileged classes, who have benefitted from colonialism, can change sides and become part of the struggle. They must be welcome in the first phase of resisting colonialism. Simply speaking, culture has complex sources of identity and dignity.[122]

Culture is the most important source of identity insofar as the social structure in which it is formed is not destroyed. Luckily for Africa, the duration of colonialism was not sufficiently long to destroy social structures, the foundational sources of what we call identity and dignity. African identities and dignities are intact, in spite of the colonial project of seeking to erase them from history. These structures serve a progressive function. Return to them is a revolutionary project, simultaneously backward- and forward-looking, a repository of the past and an expression of the possible.[123]

Cabral insists that first and foremost Africa must be cleansed from vestiges of colonialism and imperialism. Like Fanon, he argues that, sadly, the decolonization project can only be achieved by violence. Toward that goal, Cabral throws himself into the armed struggle with his brothers and sisters in Cape Verde and Guinea-Bissau, making possible the overthrow of colonialism and the attainment of independence, which he did not live to lead, although it was hoped that he would be the leader of the non-aligned movement.

Cabral believed that Marxism must be stretched and adjusted to the realities of the African continent and that Africa must seek its own autonomous socialist path.[124] He theorized possibilities for the revolutionary human condition from the perspective of the Global South but aimed at transforming the world.

For Cabral, the South can be changed only if the North also changes, and these processes must take place simultaneously. For him the African can be changed only if the human self changes everywhere. Cabral was an international revolutionary and not simply a blind provincial nationalist.

Fanon, Nkrumah, and Cabral were world figures who acted nationally but thought globally. The three of them provided the revolutionary dimension of African philosophy. In their hands philosophy becomes a material and non-material weapon of transformation of consciousness. All three were convinced that the world could change and that language in concert with consciousness, unlike post-modernist cynicisms, can expand our horizons. All three considered the human as actional, philosophical, and capable of forging new human personalities. For all three, the human is a possibility with rich imaginary resources that provide the resources for change. For them, human beings can mature in the context of time and constructive upheavals. Moreover, all three were committed to a creolized Marxist revolutionary vision of radical democracy and radical socialism.

Fanon advocated that Marxism must be stretched to embrace the role of race in the colonial project. Nkrumah adds that Marxism can be reconciled with African communities. Cabral concludes that the African must seek an autonomous socialist path in concert with a radically global socialist path.

Three of them display remarkable erudition and originality as they deeply reflect about the "African condition," but always with a global concern. Although they think within the African historical context, and about African matters, they never lose sight of the fact that Africa is part of the world, the origin of the human species, and that all that happens to Africans is deeply linked to universal struggles outside of the continent.

Fanon, Nkrumah, and Cabral are thinkers from the Global South. As thinkers from the Global South, they are committed to change the world by giving it original values, born in the South, as in Africa, yet belonging to the world. They were crucially aware that the South, home of profound values, was mistreated by the colonizers and always regarded as a data to be studied in the North, by northern thinkers, but not as the origin of values that can be diffused and shared with the North and from which new human beings can flourish. These three revolutionary thinkers were radical humanists and radical democrats.

For Fanon, theory was a cleanser of the soul, and action the motivator of the body. For him, the objectification and commodification of black people, both in the hands of whites and blacks, must end.

For Nkrumah, the African personality is a morally organized being who would not subject other human beings to unnecessary suffering through the venom of the unjustified existence of classes that exploit others, which is shameful and must be expunged by revolutionary violence.

For Cabral, philosophy itself is a material force in that a philosophically informed people seeks to know its culture, its history, its customs and traditions, and in that it can also critically distinguish cultures that impoverish the soul from cultures that enrich it and understand that what we call identities and dignities arise out of a critical examination of one's soul. The autonomous socialist path, which he chose, can come about only when Africans choose the best for the world. To Cabral, the South is a source of values, which can humanize the world.

Our age is the age of fragmentation by race, class, gender, and sexuality. These facts, as important as they are, make it impossible for human beings to organize under a core principle that cuts through the fragmentation. Fanon, Nkrumah, and Cabral were aware of the importance of recognizing the fragmentation but they were intelligently hopeful that the idea of the birth of a new human being, motivated by a passion for justice, truth, peace, and prosperity, can transcend the fragmentation of our age and replace it by the unifying idea of radical humanity.

Radical humanity can come about after the dissolution of capitalism and imperialism. The fragmentations of our time are constructions of colonialism, slavery, racism, and sexism, and they can be abolished by the activities of new revolutionary subjects from the Global South and Global North.

Existence precedes essence in the particular sense that appearances are not real because they participate in hidden essences of which they are manifestations, but precisely because they are real themselves, they exist. Race, sex, and gender are not real in that they are essences. They are real because they are partly real.

B. LEWIS GORDON ON BLACK EXISTENCE

In *Existentia Africana*, his early, brilliant book, Lewis Gordon defines philosophies of existence, of which black existence is a seminal part, as a critical engagement of philosophical questions concerned with freedom, anguish, responsibility, embodied agency, sociality, and liberation.[125] His focus is an analysis of the meaning of blackness and the experience of being black, as the two are interrelated. He begins with meaning and then draws out its direct impact on the global experiences of blacks.

Whereas Fanon was a classical analyst of the colonial world, Gordon, who closely follows but goes beyond Fanon with great modesty, is the voice of the post-colonial world, in which racism maintains its barbaric presence, long after laws have been made against it. Gordon becomes an existentialist in order to explain the lingering presence of global racism in the form of black existence. Central to his concern is the role and function of bad faith, as an explanation of why racism still retains its force in the lives of those blacks who it traumatizes in everyday life. The question which Gordon asks is why is it that after laws have been passed and apartheid has been formally abolished blackness continues to be a problem that plagues black people's lives everywhere in the world. Gordon's lifetime focus is an analysis of this perennial problem.

Gordon's early book, *Bad Faith and Anti Black Racism*, is a sustained meditation on the phenomenon of racism in the post-colonial black world. In that book, he uses the Sartrean idea of bad faith to critically understand the constancy and consistency of racism's presence in the post-colonial Global North. This theme informs the entire project of Gordon's distinct voice informed by Sartre and Fanon, and goes beyond them. There is now what we might call an original Gordonian voice on behalf of the condemned of the earth.

Summarizing his arguments over the years, Gordon, writes, "There is a simple version of my argument from those years: Racism requires denying the humanity of other groups of human beings through the organization of them, through regimes of power, under the category of a race and then denying the ascription of human being to them. The performative contradiction is that they would first have to be identified as human beings in order to deny their being such. It is thus a form of mauvaise-foi [bad faith]. Since racism is a form of mauvaise-foi, antiblack racism, as a species of racism, must also be a form of mauvaise-foi."[126]

Black existence simply means that blacks, contrary to the racists who think otherwise, appear, stand out, and are present in situations that seek to make them disappear, not stand out, or be absent. Being black is a way of saying: I am here; I stand out in situations that I choose. I am a human being, an individual with a name, a history. Do not just call me black like all other blacks. Of course, I am black like all other blacks, but I have a name and am relationally and socially alive. I must, however, fight for this identity, for this presence, which the racist, in bad faith, attempts to erase. I, as a black, must rewrite this erasure, intellectually and physically. I do the first by producing literature about and by blacks, and physically by actionality, by revolutionary violence.

In a series of interviews, Lewis Gordon, has powerfully defended black existence as human existence. For Gordon, blackness is not a substance, or a fixed ontology, but an expression of a possibility among possibilities, and also a relation with others who recognize blacks as human beings. Denying that blacks are human beings is acting in bad faith. It is the white person lying to himself. Whereas the black recognizes the white as other, therefore, as a human being, the white does not recognize the black as other, therefore, not as a human being. The denial of otherness to blacks is the most complete way of dehumanizing blacks, so that the white can do anything to them, including attempting to make blacks socially deceased. These extraordinary claims are fully and compellingly developed in *Existentia Africana*.[127] Blackness, a consequence of situated choosing and not only abstract individuality is relationality, that is, living with others as respected and fully human beings with flesh and blood. The individuality of blacks as human can only be a consequence of blacks choosing their blackness, as an act of self-designation, or self-definition, as I wish to call it. This humanity is not a material substance but a dynamic becoming. The blackness of blacks can only be recognized by whites when the racist world is dismantled by the revolutionary actionality of blacks in concert with whites, should progressive whites wish to join the movement. If whites cannot join this struggle, then blacks must do the work singularly.

This original insight is the founding principle of Lewis Gordon's work. All his books and essays are premised on this understanding of blackness and of black existence.

When we are certain that the black exists, then we face another problem, namely, the status of black productions, their very values. Everything that the black produces is considered something particular to blacks, something that is nothing, not a thing, of no value, which can be appreciated and understood only by blacks themselves as experiences, most of which have been problems. The self-theorized task of the racist is to theoretically examine the problems, which the problem people—read blacks—cannot understand. Creating problems is black and solving them is white. Black problems are experience, and white projects are solving those experiences—this structure is always a failure, only a theory, a philosophy. Black problems created by racism are treated as problems created by blacks, which can only be solved by theory. Black pathology, when there is one, is a direct consequence of physical and intellectual oppression, such as the physical abuse of the black body, as in lynching, and the foundational colonizing of the mind that convinces blacks that they cannot think—they can only be problems, the white man's burden. These illusory conceptions of the white racist are functions of bad faith. Gordon writes,

"By bad faith, I mean the effort to evade freedom, to hide from responsibility, through investment in a version of the self and reality that is not only false but also such that one seduces oneself to believe what one ultimately does not believe. While often examined at an individual level, the concept is such that it always requires a bad relationship with evidence (a very public, appearing phenomenon). To make oneself believe what one does not believe requires taking oneself out of a relationship with evidence through investing in contradictory activity such as 'non-evidential evidence,' 'relations of no relations,' and so forth. In effect, evidence, which is a social phenomenon, loses its sociality. Bad faith wages, in other words, a war against social reality. It also attacks human existence as relational."[128]

He continues, "As to exist (from Latin, ex sistere) means to stand out, to emerge, to appear, bad faith is an attitude of disappearance, either of the self or of others. In either version, there is the attempted eradication of relationality. These aspects of bad faith lead, further, to a profound struggle with the body and embodiment, for one cannot appear except through being somewhere and other things cannot appear without that to which they appear also having a point of view. In effect, then, bad faith, although studied as a condition of consciousness, is also that of the body by virtue of the inseparability of consciousness, embodiment, and freedom: it is, in other words, always bodies in bad faith, and as they live in a world sullied with incomplete selves, malleable and unmalleable things, the relation to all without seeming closure, the realization of purity as a projected ideal instead of reality."[129]

This conclusion of bad faith's attacks on relationality turns much of Western thought on its head. For Plato, as we know, was antipathetic to the shadows, which he regarded as mere appearance to be overcome through insight into purified reality.

For Gordon, black existence as opposed to black absence is a perpetual quest for a home; it is a yearning for recognition not as non-others, but as human, as Dasein, looking for a human world.

As Gordon puts it,

> To be unconstrained is not identical with freedom. To be free, one must have a place to which one belongs. One must have a home. This is an insight from early antiquity, where reflections on exile brought this point to the fore. To be released from persecution by virtue of protection in another person's home offers safety but not freedom. To be free, one must be able to appear without qualification, to appear with legitimacy, and to have justification for that appearance. That condition is the meaning of home. But home in this sense need not be a formal domicile. It could also be symbolic and epistemological. One can, for instance, achieve a form of freedom through finding one's intellectual home, one's artistic home, those elements of life that make one at home in the world (see Gordon, 2008b).[130]

Gordon is astutely right. Indeed, having a home is a sign of self-sufficiency, that one is self-respecting, hard–working, and self-determined enough to be able to have an intimate space called home. No one is allowed to enter that home without the owner's permission. It is precisely this kind of spiritual and physical ownership that the black person is not permitted to have when told that they have no home, that the world does not belong to the black person. The world is arbitrarily given to the white person, who tells blacks that they are not allowed to appear in this space. This is a space only for those who are free to come and go as they wish. At the white man's home the black can appear only as a slave, a servant, a server, a domestic, or simply as an object among objects. For those who escaped the Global South in search of making a living as exiles, home is cleaning the white man's mansions, fixing his cars, polishing his shoes at shopping malls. Home is an exilic existence of a temporary abode, from which the oppressed visitor can be kicked at will.

Home is the absence of a real home for black men and women. The absent blacks are put in non-homes, absence of home. As absents they are absent spaces, without homes. In a deeper sense, owning a home is owning yourself, being a person—a right that is also denied to women, according to de Beauvoir. The first step of owning oneself is being a human like all others. Home has many other steps, which the black person has to climb.

Home is also owning one's thoughts, one's music, one's artistic work as an expression of one's freedom to create, to choose, to cultivate through one's own transcendental gifts, and to transcend oneself, from the realm of non-being to the realm of Being, to the realm of interpreting one's experience, to produce theory, philosophy, literature, science. This freedom is also denied to blacks, as Gordon insightfully. Blacks are first placed in deplorable conditions. They are made absent, and if they are ever present, it is conditional presence. This is designated as experience, in which blacks are called problem people. Whites create these problems for blacks without homes, and then the whites, producers of ideas, will solve these problems—but they fail, with the greedy resources of the capitalist state, and then the problems linger.

Recently, Gordon astutely wrote,

> Valuing black life is no small matter. Indeed, a great deal of history was recently made by Alicia Garza, a queer black woman, simply tweeting the hashtag #BlackLivesMatter. That there are now organizations, street protests, and a body of literature studying this phenomenon across the globe attests to the degree to which a good deal of Euromodernity was committed to black lives not mattering.
>
> By "Euromodernity," I don't mean "European people." The term simply means the constellation of convictions, arguments, policies, and a worldview promoting the idea that the only way legitimately to belong to the present and as a consequence the future is to be or become European. It places "European" as a necessary condition of belonging, continuation, and selfhood—features of all Modernities—which, in effect, relegates those who do not either to the past or to kinds of nowhere and no-man's-land, what Fanon (1952) called the "zone of nonbeing." Thus any movement or theory that advances black lives belonging to the present and future violates the norms of that enterprise. Their "mattering" becomes a challenge to the secular theodicy of an epoch premised on their not mattering or, put simply, their absence.[131]

This is a moral and political project of the existentially serious self, who knows that the world is an alienating place that has put millions of human beings in miserable situations, particularly blacks and women, defined as non-persons, who exist for white males, who masquerade as free, human, complete, normal, and as standards of human excellence. I will return to this theme in the final chapters of this book, when I address the issues of self-construction and self-definition.

C. PAGET HENRY AND AFRICAN ONTOLOGY

Ontology is the study of Being, existence and becoming, and Africans have held their commitment to ontology far longer than their Western counterparts. African ontology as part of African philosophy has continued to organize African life since it came into being as early as 2500 years ago.

Ancient Egyptian thinkers have contributed mightily to the birth and maturity of ontology as an important part of philosophy. Ancient Egypt, an African civilization, gave the world its first systematic ontology symbolized by the idea of Nun, the liquid ether from which emerged the ancient transcendent, Atum Ra, who in turn functioned as the supreme reality, the originator of space and time, and thus the universe.[132] Atum Ra was the divine grounding of the universe, the cosmos, earth and sky, and human order itself.

Professor Paget Henry humbly acknowledges the formative role of African foundational writers on whom he builds, by writing, "long before there were professors of philosophy there were philosophers. Gyekye and Oruka in particular have developed for us the role of the African sages who were the producers of rich philosophical traditions."[133]

Professor Paget Henry is among the foremost thinkers who have systematically articulated this ontology, as one of the pillars of Afro-Caribbean philosophy. His penetration of African ontology is premised on the original view that Caribbean philosophy needs an ontological grounding and that African philosophy can readily provide one, provided that the Caribbean thinker plumbs the past, so as to unravel the hidden ontology of her distant and immediate African thinkers. Henry does so through a philosophical idiom which does not relegate African ontology merely to an exercise in Ethnophilosophy,[134] but uses the crucial ethnographic data as a potent source as he develops a philosophy of African religions embedded in a discussion of the structure of Supreme Being, therefore an analysis of ontology as a part of philosophy, as it applies to the African condition.

Henry introduces this daunting task of presenting African ontology by writing: "The vision that informs traditional African philosophy, that generates its fundamental questions is a religious one."[135]

Henry is right. It is precisely the religions' horizons that provide the ontology, and the ontology itself can then be further engaged through the devices of analytic philosophy and the resources of existential phenomenology.

African religions and their ontologies are similar to Eastern philosophy, in which the religion informs the philosophy, and the philosophy in turn generates the ontology. Indeed, Brahmin, a supreme reality, functions exactly like Atum Ra in Egyptian/African philosophy.[136] Brahmin and Atum Ra are the originators of the universe. One could extend this insight to include numerous other African ontologies, as we shall see below. Henry argues that these two are originators of cosmonogicontologies, as Henry dubs it.

The rest of this chapter is a detailed elaboration of the above thesis. I will argue, following Henry, for the thesis that in African religions, as for example among the Igbo's of Eastern Nigeria, there is a Supreme Being who creates the universe and is in turn self-created, and is luminous and self-organizing. For the Igbos, this Supreme Being created the earth and sky and also two messengers, the moon and the sun, who report on the African condition. Similarly, among the Yorubas of Nigeria, the creator god shares his ashe, or generative powers, with the animal kingdom, which includes a python, a viper, a snail, an earthworm, and a woodpecker.[137]

Africans draw their identities by embedding their existence in a luminous, self-creating and self-organizing Supreme Being who gives Africans the attribute of existence so that they can give a rational accounting of their existence and the cause of their existence. Their identity is deeply linked with the self-generating Supreme Being who consciously created them by sharing his powers with them and all the other beings, including animals and plants with which they share the world. In this view, all beings are created by the Supreme Being and all these beings have dignity and corresponding rights, which cannot be violated. These sacred dignities are the sources of African existential seriousness. These mythopoeic articulations of African existence are simultaneously mythical and rational, descriptive and analytical, poetic and discursive. Their very mythicality is the source of a rationality that mystified a litany of Western anthropologists and some reductionist Africans, who themselves jettisoned these ontologies as ethnophilosophy and rejected their philosophical status.

Henry has brilliantly restored the purity and power of these mythopoeic ontologies, which are also articulated in analytic proverbs as in classical Ethiopian philosophy.[138] These ontologies are sources of African identity. Through them Africans are given complete individual ontologies, which also link them to the communities in which they grow and mature. In this view, the African conception of the individual is imbedded in community, and the community itself is composed of ontologically complete individuals who move from the *I* to the *we*, and when necessary, from the *we* to the *I*. African ontological vocabularies empower individuals to speak as free individuals, critically and lovingly.

Thanks to Paget Henry, these ontologies are now reclaiming their eminent philosophical value. These African narratives of creation are the precise sources of African ontologies. Being, as a supreme reality, which created itself and the universe, cannot be understood outside the Cosmo-ontologies. The

African self-understanding is that individual Africans only exist because the Supreme Being is sharing his ashe with all those whom he created. Individuals exist to the precise extent that they partake in the ashe of the Supreme Being who endowed them individually with the attribute of existence by which they propagate the human species as biological beings. There is no duality in this narrative. Being and beings, subject and object interpenetrate. Individual beings exist only because they partake in the ashe bestowed on them by the creator Being. The ego is pervaded by the Supreme Being who expands African horizons of being by embedding them in a being who gives Africans a sense of their immanence. In this view, transcendence and immanence interpenetrate in the generation of a spiritually conscious African personality. The African personality is deeply spiritual, and this spirituality is precisely what is needed to control the material excesses of the ego's desires. The excesses are regulated by the abundant spirituality, which guides moral action. okra is to the African soul as reason is to the soul, as Plato following his Egyptian thinkers observed. Okra is as equally universalizable, except that okra is a product of the South and has not been given the attention it deserves by Northern philosophers. Otherwise, okra just as easily could be the organizing principle of individual souls on a Global scale.

Of course, philosophers from the Global South, of whom Henry is a foremost leader, are changing the nature of the discourse. Thanks to Paget Henry and Lewis Gordon, two hard-working philosophical voices of the Global South, the Global South is now emerging not merely as a depository of Euro-American discourse but as a source of universalizing values, now that the geography of reason has shifted to the Global South: the cradle of human civilization.

For the Bantus of the Belgian Congo, the Supreme Being is perceived as pure force. Exactly like the Yoruba Supreme Being, who inhabits the physical universe in the form of ashe, so does this Supreme Being impart to those whom he created an enabling and empowering force. Individual human beings are suffused with a vital force, which gives potency and agency. Force for the Bantus and ashe for the Yorubas empower Africans to make things happen, to generate change and transformation.

The same is true for the Akans of Ghana. For the Akans, the African person is made up of three inseparable parts, very much like the three inseparable parts of the human soul (reason, spirit, and desire) for Plato. According to Akan ontology, the human person is composed of okra (soul), sumsum (ego) and the homan (body). Following Gyekye, the individual person is an "ontic unity." The okra is a divine gift from the Supreme Being, Onayame, who exists in all human beings, as it is for the Igbos, the Yorubas, and the Bantus. The sumsum must follow the spiritual paths divinized by okra in order to achieve human fulfillment. Similarly, the homan must also follow the regulations of sumsum carved out by okra, in order to live a life of balance and moderation by following the standards of excellence lovingly suggested by okra. Through this systematic scheme, the African individual becomes ontologically complete and moral life becomes a definite possibility. This ontic unity seamlessly produces a balanced human being, destined to live the good life. As Paget puts it, "This spiritual order was central to the African religious visions of existence in this way, the ontologically complete individual African maps out an existentially serious moral life" (Henry 2000, 25).

For Paget, African ontology directly leads to the production of cosmogonicontology. The different Supreme Beings among African cultures are represented by a plethora of images and attributes. Thus, for the Akans, Onayame is represented as alone, absolute, the eternal, boundless architect and originator: uncreated, omniscient, and omnipotent. These are attributes of perfection.

Among the Igbos, Chineke, is described through similar properties. The Supreme Beings of these different cultures are also the creators of space—of the universe itself. In this sense, Paget argues the ontology is simultaneously cosmogony.

For Paget, African ontology is intimately connected to an examination of existence and leads to a discussion of existential seriousness.

Ontology is also the study of existence: the existence of humans and external objects. African ontology is particularly sensitive to the existence of humans and the conditions in which they exist. Ethics is singularly focused on the conditions of human existence. The African moral philosopher dissects the human status of existence. Thus, it is important that we recognize human beings as bearers of rights that cannot be violated. When any right is violated, the existence of that individual shouts out for unconditional attention. The existentially serious moral philosopher is committed to the documentation of cases in which individual rights are transgressed and blatantly violated.

The existential rights of the individual are guided by the ontologically determined status of the individual person in the eyes of the Supreme Beings, which guide everyday African life. The individual is not only a self-determining ego but also, importantly, a spiritual being with a destiny; a destiny mapped out for the person by the spiritual forces. In this view existence is not immanent, but transcendent. It is not self-determining but rather a coherently organized ontic structure beholden to a transcendental power—the power of the deities who lead the individual. The life of the individual is ontologically determined, but existentially dynamic. The individual determines her destiny in concert with guidance furnished by the Supreme Beings of the various African cultures.

Paget writes, "There is an inherent tendency in the SUMSUM to revolt against the cosmic order of things and subject it to its own creative and self-creative powers. This tendency to revolt on the part of the ego is very clearly captured in the Dogon myth of the struggle between Yurugu and Amma, the creator God. Yurugu is a classic figure of cosmic discord, like the Judeo-Christian counterpart, Lucifer."[139]

The crisis-ridden ego is then softly guided by the deities to respect the internal relation of sumsum with okra, the regulatory spiritual force, and is challenged to respect its spiritual leaders. It is in this sense that ontology provides the Self to examine its existence critically, in order to free itself from permanent crisis.

The ego is at all times expected, and spiritually trained, to submit to the existential paths carved out for it by the all-knowing deities who gave the ego the precious attribute of contingent existence. And unless the ego is to be pervaded by permanent crisis, it must humbly submit to its fate and perform the necessary duties of stable existence.

The ego must respect that it is a coherently organized ontic entity embedded in a restructured ontological reality guided by spiritual beings that created beings, of which humans are one.

Again, Henry writes: "In contrast to Indian traditions that call for a dissolving of the ego into the Atman, or soul, African solutions to the problems of ego existence call not for its spiritual dissolution, but for each individual ego to recognize its unique spiritually encoded nature and the responsibilities that come with it. This affirmation of ego existence is thus a primary contribution to African existentialism to philosophical anthropology. If the cosmogonic discourses of African philosophy revealed its celestial reach, then its existential discourses reveal its human depths. Between the two, we get a good look at the comprehensive nature of traditional African philosophy."[140]

I would like to end the chapter by extracting three analytic propositions from the above ontological discussions thus far:

(1)
The ego's existence is owed to the Deities.
Okra is the divining grounding of sumsum.
Therefore, Sumsum must follow its divine grounding, its okra.

(2)
The ego unnecessarily creates a crisis for itself.
This crisis is self-caused.
Therefore, the crisis can be solved only if the ego follows its destiny, its predestination in the order of things.

(3)
That the ego will always exist as an ontic entity.
The ego cannot become one with its creators.

As a created ontic reality, it occupies a different space of reality. The space that it occupies is inferior to the space of the deities. Therefore, what the deities order, given their place, must be obeyed.

D. BELL HOOKS, THE BLACK WOMAN

bell hooks, a famed black feminist, has been examining the situation of the black woman. Whereas Gordon and Henry focused on the existence and relationality of blacks, bell hooks's task was to engage in a critical analysis of blackness and womanhood simultaneously. The existence of blacks as absence is also true of the black woman, who is absent by virtue of her blackness, peculiarly absent, also, in the eyes of men and white women. Working class black women carry the added value of class to the multiple sources of their oppression. White women in particular make the black woman absent by excluding her as a thinker and actional in the global feminist project. Consequently, the black woman has to articulate a black feminist project, of which hooks is a prominent voice.

bell hooks convincingly argues that black woman is oppressed both because of her blackness, which she shares with the black man, and her womanness, which she shares with women universally. She is also in tension with white women, because of their whiteness, and she battles black men, because of black masculinity. Indeed, the situation of the black woman is truly complex. bell hooks is a foremost analyst of this complex edifice of the black woman's Self.

She writes,

> This knowledge seems especially important at this historical moment when black women, and other women of color, have worked to create awareness of the ways in which racism empowers white women to act as exploiters and oppressors. . . . By calling attention to interlocking systems of domination—sex, race, and class—black women and many other groups of women acknowledge the diversity and complexity of female experience, of our relationship to power and domination. The intent is not to dissuade people of color from becoming engaged in feminist movement. Feminist struggle to end patriarchal domination should be of primary importance to women and men globally not because it is the foundation of all other oppressive structures but because it is that form of domination we are most likely to encounter in an ongoing way in everyday life.[141]

The message is that in spite of the complexity of the particularity of the multifaceted oppression of the black woman, the feminist struggle to end male domination must lead the way. For now, that is the primary struggle, the other struggles are secondary struggles. White and black men's oppression of women under the tutelage of the masculine gaze, as de Beauvoir and Butler argued, must be the center of the struggle to end masculine domination. In hooks's own words, "Feminist effort to end patriarchal domination should be of primary concern because it insists on the eradication of exploitation and oppression in the family context and in all other intimate relationships."[142]

The black woman of working class background, such as hooks, is oppressed by the central forces of class, race, sex, and gender. Four pillars of oppression stand in her way. Sex and gender must be stretched to include class and race, in order to adequately understand the particularity and uniqueness of the black woman from a working-class background.

The black woman is subjected to pain also. hooks writes movingly, "In my case, I was hit by my companion at a time in life when a number of forces in the world outside our home had already 'hit' me, so to speak, made me painfully aware of my powerlessness, my marginality. It seemed that I was confronting being black and female and without money in the worst possible ways."[143]

Note how seamlessly bell hooks blends the intricate weaving of race, class, and gender as they conspire against her, even when she is fully conscious of her deplorable condition environed by pain, and yet cannot be actional. At first, her critical self-consciousness is suffocated by paralysis. She cannot choose an exit from this situated freedom, in which she can only dream that she is free. Her actionality is indeed propelled toward feminism as a viable exit strategy. She chose to be free, and acting on that freedom became a self-founded emancipatory project with other black women in a similar situation. Her actionality is exemplary.

This description fits the conditions of hundreds of women. Some are hit repeatedly. Others sporadically. Still others, sufficiently enough to merit attention, which they rarely do. Afraid that they will be labelled as battered women, and in addition, stay in bad situations, they stay and suffer, along with their children, some of whom are abused also. bell hooks exposes this data as a project for feminism.

The intersection of race, class, and sex that surrounds the black woman's life can be overcome only when the organizing principle is love, love as the empowering force that must convince men and women that in order to live fully and realize human possibilities for all the victims of oppression, patriarchy must be ended.[144]

At the center of this patriarchy is the masculine gaze that surveys the black woman's body and decides to abuse it at will, since this body is considered non-being, non-person, non-relational, not even ontologically present. It is an absence, whose non-being calls for enslavement, colonization, and violence in the hands of an oppressed black husband, lover, and partner. Not even the intimate space, home, is spared of this violence, this pain, which traumatizes its victims forever.

bell hooks has decided to tell it all, to be the voice of the private sphere and to relocate this sphere in the public sphere, for scrutiny by the human gaze of compassion and of love, leading to actionality in the form of feminism.[145]

NOTES

93. Frantz Fanon, *Black Skin, White Masks* (New York: Grove Press, 1967), 17.
94. Lewis Gordon, *What Fanon Said* (New York: Fordham University Press, 2015).
95. Fanon, *Black Skin, White Masks* 12.
96. Ibid., 109.
97. Ibid., 111–12.
98. Ibid., 109.
99. Ibid., 8.
100. Obenga, *Egypt and Ancient Africa*.
101. Fanon, *Black Skin, White Masks*, 140.
102. Ibid., 141–99.
103. Ibid., 154.
104. Fanon, *Wretched of the Earth*, 35.
105. Ibid., 94.
106. Ibid., 45.
107. Ibid., 123.
108. Frantz Fanon, *A Dying Colonialism* (New York: Grove Press, 1965). In this book, Fanon probes the anatomy of the Algerian revolution by examining the Algerian family, the role of the media, medicine and revolutionary psychiatry.
109. Jane Gordon, *Creolizing Political Theory: Reading Rousseau Through Fanon* (New York: Fordham University Press, 2014). Gordon brilliantly presents Fanon as a theorist of direct democracy together with Jean-Jacques Rousseau.
110. *The Wretched of the Earth*, 148–207. Neil Robert's *Marronage* (New York: Fordham University Press, 2015) is a great read and its brilliant chapter on violence is highly engaging.
111. Ibid., 205.
112. Ibid., 206–48.
113. Ibid., 246.
114. Kwame Nkrumah, *Consciencism* (New York: Monthly Review Press, 1964), 63. This book is a synthesis of Nkrumah's major philosophical and political writings.
115. Ibid., 95.
116. Ibid., 98.
117. Ibid., 103.

118. Amilcar Cabral, *Return to The Source* (New York: Monthly Review Press, 1973), 53.
119. Ibid., 38–41.
120. Ibid., 43–45.
121. Ibid., 436–53.
122. Ibid., 69.
123. Ibid., 60–67.
124. Reiland Rabaka, *Concepts of Cabralis,* (Lanham, MD: Lexington Books, 2014). For a comprehensive analysis of Cabral's revolutionary theory see this text. Rabaka's footnotes are remarkably rich for a mastery of Cabral's theories of revolution.
125. Lewis Gordon, *Existensia Africana* (New York: Routledge, 2000), 10.
126. Lewis R. Gordon, "Thoughts on two recent decades of studying race and racism," Social Identities (2017) DOI: 10.1080/13504630.2017.1314924.
127. Gordon, *Existentia Africana*, 85.
128. Gordon, *Is Philosophy Blue?*, 15.
129. Ibid., 17.
130. Lewis Gordon, *Black Existence in Philosophy of Culture,* Diogenes 59, nos. 3–4 (2014), 96–105, ICPHS 2013.
131. Lewis Gordon, "Creolizing critical pedagogy and political theories of education," *Review of Education, Pedagogy, and Cultural Studies*, 40, no. 1, 2017.
132. Theophille Obenga, "Egypt: Ancient History of African Philosophy," in *A Companion to African Philosophy*, ed. Kwasi Wiredu (Hoboken, NJ: Blackwell Publishers, 2004).
133. Paget Henry, *Caliban's Reason: Introducing Afro-Caribbean Philosophy* (London: Routledge, 2000), 21.
134. The early Houtondji had dismissed ethnophilosophy as nonphilosophical. Henry's Caliban's Reason is a sustained response to this dismissal.
135. Henry, *Caliban's Reason*, 23. See also Kwame Gyekye, *An Essay on African Philosophical Thought: The Akan Conceptual Scheme* (Cambridge, UK: Cambridge University Press, 1987).
136. Ibid., 23.
137. Ibid., 23.
138. Teodros Koros, *Zara Yacob: On the Rationality of the Human Heart* (Trenton, NJ: Africa World Press, 2002).
139. Ibid., 32.
140. Ibid., 37.
141. bell hooks, *Talking Back* (Boston: South End Press, 1989), 21.
142. Ibid., 22.
143. Ibid. 85.
144. Ibid., 27.
145. Ibid., 35–42, 17–83.

• 11 •

Self-Definition

A. Self-Construction
B. Imagination
C. Possibilities
D. Norms
E. Values
F. Reason
G. Faith

The last eleven chapters were guided by the idea of self-definition. The Self is a composite of possibilities. Possibilities are enabling values that empower the Self as it yearns for freedom to choose, to create, to evaluate and then settle on a particular vision that makes it a human Self.

By self-definition, I propose a human being freely choosing, as opposed to being imposed on, as fulfilling aesthetics and ethics of existence in the primordial zones of being—sex, race, and gender. When any person is choosing a sexual orientation, or any form of identity, that person is defining a Self. These three zones of being are expressions of the Self when it freely and confidently identifies itself with a race, a sexual orientation, and a gender. In this argument, race and sexual orientation are not biological impositions on the Self, but freely chosen appearances of Being, deliberately chosen modes of Being, and wise articulations of an ethics of conscious existence. The appearances themselves are real only when they are freely chosen by the consciously free Self, otherwise, they are nothing more than imposed forms of non-being to which the person submits in order to avoid stigmas and insults by the heterosexual community of self-appointed judges. When a person is imposed on in this way, they are being forced to be what they do not feel, or what they do not want to be. It is the road of inauthenticity, guided by bad faith. This Self, unlike Dasein, is not a question. It is a possibility that is chosen in the realm of the unknowable nature of the Self, known to itself and to others in a similar condition, to the extent that composites can be known.

Race, sex, and gender are not simple, in the sense that the indivisible, indestructible, and deathless soul is—as Plato effectively argued in *The Phaedo,* or as *The Upanishads* contend in their characterization of Brahman. Race, sex, and gender, although freely chosen, are in fact divisible and perishable. What is particular about self-definition is that the sex, race, and gender that we wear are attempts at defining ourselves, instead of being ontologically fixed by biology and anatomy. We find ourselves determined by biology, as a man, as a woman, as a male or female. But external characterizations of the Self are not founded by the Self, instead, we find ourselves in these predetermined destinies. The idea of self-definition punctures this balloon of fixed ontology.

The authentic Self that lives in good faith, is simple. It does not hide anything. It lives its life with all of life's complexities and ambiguities. The authentic choice does not necessarily lead to happiness, to a life without disappointments. What matters is that the Self has freely chosen within situatedness. Life will always be impregnated with disappointments as we steadily move toward death, to another life in the form of death but with the possibility of deathlessness—as we learned from ancient Egypt, Plato, and the Christian thinkers.

The first vision of the Self, as I argued in the first chapter, is that of the ancient Egyptian Nun, a dynamic, water-like but not water, material strata, which according to the ancient Egyptian thinkers was the beginning of everything that is. Call it Being, material being, a kind of substance, which simply is there. This Nun in turn created the first god, Atum Ra.

I would like to contemporize this idea as the first primordial definition of the Self. This Self is sex, race, and gender neutral. If the ancient Egyptians were right, and evidence and argumentation have proved them so, as Obenga contended, then we have the first act of a self-defining Being, which is not fixed ontologically but willing and able to cultivate humans who can choose to be from any race, are of undetermined sex, and undetermined gender. All that there is is a Being who can develop possibilities of sex, race, and gender. This Being is a silent creator of all that is, including others with the capacity to style a life and determine forms born out of freedom, and develop the facets of existence as they live, grow, and move toward another life free of the seeming permanence of bodily existence.

This insight is reinforced in the *Upanishads* and *Gita* as well. The Brahman of the *Upanishads* and in the great epic, *Gita*, is also sex and gender neutral. We are informed in both texts that Brahman is imperishable and cannot be present to the bodily senses. Although Brahman created beings with bodies, Brahman itself does not have a body but is present in all beings. The beings in which it is present can choose their possibilities, and therefore, define themselves, if they wish, as man or woman, male or female. Brahman can accommodate the wishes and inclinations of all those whom it has created. Exactly as does Atum Ra, Brahman also creates others in order that they can recreate themselves with the anatomies that they are born in. This is a creation toward a potentiality with an impermanent actuality.

Brahman is not a person with bodily characteristics. It is a Being that is subject to change and ultimate death. I can therefore draw from these two master texts that Being, itself, is sex neutral, and the beings created in Brahman's image are also sex neutral. They are there only with a raw form, awaiting human completion, human attendance, and committed and enlightened fulfillment. The actualities might as well be only dreams, as Chuang Tzu contended earlier in the argument.

When we move to the China of Chuang Tzu, the expressions of self-definition are starkly radical. For him values are relational, that is, relative to each other. Thus, cold is not the opposite of hot, but cold is rather that which is not hot, or that which is hot but appears to be cold. In human life, being alive is not the opposite of being dead. Rather, being alive is one form of being, relative to being dead, which is another form of being that is being alive. Thus, hot and cold, life and death, being awake and dreaming are not absolutes. They are not only relative to each other, but part of the flow of being. Being, like Nun, is dynamic, ever-flowing, moving, and becoming.

Race, sex, and gender in this sense are also not absolutes. They are the possibilities of being, that is being's temporary forms. In fact, they might just be dreams, which we habitually confuse with permanent actuality. The actual is just a dream. Simon de Beauvoir is right that there is no woman, one becomes a woman. One is not fixed to be born as a woman, or a man, or transgender. These are merely appearances or potential actualities. These are forms of being, given by Being, and Being itself is all forms, none of the forms, or present in all forms. Nothing is beyond Being, and everything is in Being.

My organizing principle is that there are no men or women, unless these categories are self-chosen within situatedness, rather, we become men and women. We are all culturally trained to play the roles of men and women, and we can in equal part culturally and religiously become re-socialized to become otherwise.

Race, sex, and gender, in this view, are appearances that the Self wears as it develops a style of existence, human existence, of which black existence, white existence, brown existence, yellow existence are particular attempts at living life. They are stylistics and ethics of self-definitions.

These attempts at self-definitions become rigid ontologies among some of the Greek philosophers. As we learned from Plato in particular, in the *Phaedo*, appearances begin to become fixed properties of the Self. There are tensions and disagreements among the symposiasts in the *Phaedo*, (as I argued in the section on Plato), but Plato takes an established position and does not offer a radical critique of the binaries—perhaps afraid of tradition and the powers that be. He ends up giving us the rigid categories of his time and disregards the philosophical views of the dissenters, who were offering sex-neutral possibilities for human beings.

The binaries of race, sex, and gender are now fully embraced, and creativities and possibilities of being human are impoverished, leading modernist writers such as Heidegger, de Beauvoir, Sartre, Fanon, Cabral, Foucault, Butler, Gordon, Henry, hooks, and many others to question these categories, from within the European world.

In this book, I join the efforts of these thinkers, but I make modest attempts to look back to ancient Egypt, India, and China to reinvigorate possibilities of being human without getting boxed in by the rigid ontologies of Eurocentrism. I try to draw out the rich resources of the Global South and open new horizons of neglected possibilities in which the Self is race, sex, and gender neutral.

A. SELF-CONSTRUCTION

In my book, *Self-Construction and the Formation of Human Values: Truth, Language and Desire* (Praeger, 1999), I distinguished three forms of constructing values, which I called:

A. Imitation
B. Modeling
C. Self-Construction.

I will now apply these distinctions to the project of self-definition, as I understand it.

Constructing something such as a value or a norm involves assembling, making, and originating. On first blush, it appears that assembling, making, and originating are so technical that only geniuses could engage them. In fact, they are not as prohibitively difficult as experts think they are. Any reasonably educated and intuitively sharp human knows the differences and can critically and judiciously distinguish them with ease. All that one needs is common sense, to know when one is imitating, (following models), and to be willing and capable of making, originating, and assembling experiences from which the individual can fashion a style of life that fits one's temperament and inclinations.

I would like to suggest that there are three forms of construction:

A. Imitation
B. Modeling
C. Self-Construction

Of these three it is (C) Self-Construction that is directly relevant to elucidating the idea of self-definition. Self-definition is mediated by self-construction, in the realm of defining oneself by consciously choosing a sexual orientation and racial identification. Defining oneself is an activity of constructing a life with a sexual orientation and the corresponding gender. Unlike (A) Imitation, which is a passive activity, and natural to the Self in that what we call learning is premised on imitating what is there, whatever the *there* is. For our purposes the *there* is, for example, the men and women whose being is ontologically fixed, those who have become men and women, in that they are there so we can imitate them as men and women. Monkeys do what they see.

A long tradition since Aristotle disagreeing with his teacher Plato, who was critical of imitation as a description of an image of images, such as the chair out there on a canvas that seeks to imitate the idea of a chair without really getting it—has assumed that humans are imitative beings, without justification. Aristotle, on the other hand, rescues the value of imitation by arguing that what is being and can be imitated is not an idea but rather an action, as in a tragic play. A play is successful when it fulfills the criteria of having a character, a plot, a spectacle, a style, an action, and a thought. Imitation has a central role to play in so far it completely integrates the six elements in the production of the play. Aristotle is right as far as he goes, but that is not far enough. His insights apply to fictionalized narratives, but my concern is not fiction. My concern is real lives that humans are struggling to live without restrictions of any kind, save the raw anatomy in which the body is enclosed.

For me, as a heterosexual man, however, the imitation of the lives of men or women poses serious limitations. Of course, I happen to be a male because I feel what I have become. Other men may not feel what they have become. They might have decided to adjust, for all kinds of reasons. In everyday lives, we are accustomed to assume that being a man or woman is a natural category that we must imitate in order to live normally. This normalcy, however, comes at a price, in that we cannot live according to how we feel, but only according to how others, the "they," as Heidegger called them, expect us to live. This normalcy is certainly becoming questioned, which is a major step toward self-definition, but not as openly as it must be. Imitating the normal restricts the range and quality of possibilities that one can choose. To a significant degree, imitation imposes unnecessary boundaries on the Self by narrowing the imaginations of the Self. The Self is now unconsciously trapped. Those who feel that they are women in a man's body still find themselves hiding. They do not come out in the open to live authentically. Authentic living is rarely encouraged in contemporary society.

Society has even coined a normalizing language for those who cannot live their lives openly. They are encouraged to hide in "the closet." I think this is a crime against humanity. Nobody should hide in the closet. If heterosexuals freely live their lives, why shouldn't homosexuals be encouraged to do the same. Of course neither heterosexuals nor homosexuals should seek to convert one another. The decision of choosing a style of existence should be executed freely and lovingly. I realize that there are too many *shoulds* in my argument, which I cannot help, because there are so many of us who are either hiding in closets, or arrogantly promoting one sexual orientation or race, or a combination of both, at the expense of others.

Individuals are increasingly becoming like commodities who sell themselves to the image that they believe will give them money and visibility. They submit to images on TV, film, and soap operas in which the Self is quartered into sexual orientations and gender roles, and the vulnerable types take the images as real and attempt to reproduce them. This is the kind of imitation that Plato was attacking, as I also did in my book, *Self-Construction and the Formation of Human Values; Truth, Language, and Desire*. The reproduction is that which is not fully thought, since it is based on imitation. Thus, some decide to become women, or men, not because they authentically feel so, but because they think that they should, because a certain celebrity whom they admire has recently decided that he thinks that he is bisexual.

This discussion now leads to the limitations of (B) modeling. Note that the person who decided that he is gay is justifying his decision upon learning through the media that the celebrity whom he admires has made that decision. The person has not independently decided to become gay because he feels that he is gay. There may be situations in which that might be the case. This is an empirical question, which deserves a study. I am here advancing a hypothesis.

Modeling his life after the celebrity robs him of his uncompromisable power to think for himself, and by himself. I call this the absence of self-definition. It is of course possible that the person has both chosen a model, and did it thoughtfully. If that is the case, then my argument, that this decision does not exemplify self-definition, is not true. My argument is compelling only when the person has modeled himself without constructing a value on his own but has internalized another person's value and diminished his freedom to choose for himself a sexual orientation and a self-founded gender.

In this example, we learn that critical thinking is absent, and passive submission to the power of the image and the authority of celebrities as models is present, and that sexual orientation is being adopted as a consequence of modeling lifestyles after that of another. The one who is modeling himself after a celebrity thus renounces his agency when he uncritically accepts a sexual orientation just because a renowned somebody has done so. Let us complicate the matter more. Consider that the model who is being imitated is a virtuous fellow, that he is a moral figure like Martin Luther King, Jr., who stands for the best in us all. Should we not then encourage those who admire this figure to do so? Several responses could be made on this case. First, (A) that it is admirable that someone has chosen the right moral cause—fighting for oppressed blacks as embedded in King. The admiration is right, but not the way it is being processed. Namely, that one is still imitating someone else, irrespective of the motive. Second, in order for (A) to be compelling, the person who has chosen King must herself, independently of the admired King, think through what King stood for and believed in it and then look for a soulmate in King. Third, it is only then that (A) can be said to move from raw imitation to conscious modeling.

That it is natural for human beings to learn by imitation is a truism. It is equally natural that we look for models to stylize our own lives, but that we should always do so is contestable. When any person begins to think for herself she can become critical of her choices, when she realizes that they are her own, and that if she was really thinking, she could have chosen otherwise. Learning through modeling, therefore, can only be the first step of exercising agency and practicing freedom. Authentic agency must necessarily go beyond the first step.

Strictly speaking, modeling itself is reliant on imitation; for the modeler is actively looking for something to model himself after. By so doing, the person is making himself a duplicate of a fixed sexual orientation, of an admired model. To that precise extent, modeling shares a crucial feature with imitation, namely, passivity of thinking, insofar as an action is being imitated with limited thought. This limitation of thought is sometimes removed when the modeler makes a conscious effort to choose among many things from which he could choose, with care and deliberation.

Modeling is also dangerous in a deep sense, and this is the case when the models we choose are blatantly bad, and when we are drawn toward vices, such as racism, sexism, and classism. Here someone must intervene to critique the choice. The critic could be a teacher, a professor, or a priest. It is the duty of those who know better to educate the misguided person to (A) think about his choice, (B) seek counseling when needed, and then (C) make a concerted effort to change. This particular possibility needs our crucial attention, if we are in fact serious about changing facets of the human condition.

Therefore, it is only when the person goes beyond imitating blindly, or as with modeling, choosing anything that is available in movies, films, TV shows, or music without exercising deep thought, that modeling too could become a dangerous source of self-construction. This kind of self-construction constricts the possibilities of the imagination to be used positively.

Self-construction, which is the third way of self-definition, unlike imitation and modeling, is always guided by deep thought and relies on the imagination and autonomous reasoning in the construction of values that empower. Furthermore, imitation and modeling share the feature of the absence of the construction of values that empower the person who is choosing under the conditions of freedom, guided by the imagination. The rest of this chapter addresses this theme in several steps.

B. IMAGINATION

Imagination is one of our powerful resources in the process of self-constructing values that helps us to shape our natural inclinations based on our anatomy.[146] The anatomy is a given. As humans, we come to this world with certain anatomies, such as our sexual organs. Some beings have penises, others have vaginas. These structures seem to be designed to perform certain functions. The aim of these structures is to produce babies who will reproduce the human species. These structures, however, are not destinies. There will always be men who will be attracted to men like them, or to both men and women; there will always be women who will be attracted to women like them, or again, to both men and women. Some will be asexual and prefer total abstention.

Anatomy is really not destiny. It is sex, gender, and race neutral. Years of cultural interpretations guided by power and wealth, however, have made anatomy our destiny. The imagination, however, can help us to rethink this enculturation, free us from submitting to the rigidities of anatomy, and to interpret our biological Self to correspond with our perceived gender roles, in which we assign gender tasks to our sexual orientations anchored in our anatomy.

If we free our imaginations and passions from the existing design of race, sex, and gender, and freely choose what we can become, and how we reconfigure our assigned anatomies, we can imagine an alternative use of our anatomies themselves.

Our anatomy is nothing more than a description of our bodily parts. It is a detailed examination of what the parts can do and cannot do. It maps out descriptions of potential structures and functions. The imagination is precisely what the person needs to exercise agency as one struggles to find her own voice in the yearning for cultivating a sexual orientation, a racial identity, or a gender role. All these performances are products of the imagination, only, if all of us are willing to consult this faculty. The faculty is there, readily potent, to serve our dreams and passions.

Imagination is the language of our inner lives. Without its use, we will be stuck in the established reality of a capitalist society that commodifies us, by selling us celebrities, sexist and racist models that many of us imitate. Imagination, when properly used, aids us in challenging the established reality with alternative realities, with possibilities. Our inner lives and passions cannot be exhausted by the established reality, which constricts our powers of what we can be, when we think freely and courageously. The very search for a sexual orientation as an act of self-construction, with imitation as the first step, and looking for models as a second step, cannot be done without the role of imagination. It is imagination, itself, which shows the person who is at the imitative and modeling stages that these two stages are inadequate, because they are still anchored in rituals and traditions, which must themselves be interrogated by the imaginative Self.

The imagination boosts the self to yearn for more and more, until the Self settles on a sexual orientation and a gender role that she authentically finds is a true home, where feeling and reason work harmoniously. The feeling that person incubates is a fulfillment of what at one point was only a dream. The imagination converts that dream into a reality, a consummation of an imagined possibility, which has now become an actuality, an existence, a concrete life, a lived practice of freedom.

The imagination gives the Self a home, chosen out of many possible homes, which the person singles out as her intimate own—one's own situated choice. In this sense, if we let the imagination guide us, it can take us to unknown zones of being, to places and sites of Being, where we can originate new ways of using our bodies and expanding the spheres of our sexual and racial inventions, by listening to the language of the body and engaging the non-bodily—thought as such—to work with the feelings produced by the body. The imagination can further empower us to train thought and body to work harmoniously, to construct new ways of being—radically new uses of our anatomy—and to open up the rigid structural and functional tasks that tradition and power have arbitrarily assigned as destiny.[147]

It is imagination that makes it possible for us to invent ourselves. The invention of the Self will be a major focus of my concluding remarks.

C. POSSIBILITIES

It is the imagination that produces possibilities. In fact, that is its central task, or so I think it should be. I would like to draw from my writerly observations of children to exemplify the suggestion that imagination can and should produce possibilities for the s=Self, as it seeks to define its being in the world.

Kindergartners are anxiously lined up to be the first to enter the classroom. It is done with style. They are calm, when they want to be, and when they can and decide to be so. They do not kick each other out. Rather, the quickest at that specific time manages to be the first in line. I notice that it is always the boys who want to be first. The girls seem not to bother. A few, like the boys, want to be first also, and they are, but generally, they have better things to do. They prefer to stay put. At times, they seem like they are laughing at these boys for making much out of this business of being the first. So, they watch the boys with great amazement. They look amused, also. It is a scene to watch. I am one of those parents who is watching the scene with great interest. This happens every morning. I look forward to it.

I must ask myself, why? Is this learned behavior picked up at home, on television, videos, friends, and from numbers of other places? I do not have absolute answers, only speculations. Where did the boys learn this obsession of being the first in line?

There are so many hard headed biologists who insist that this aggressiveness is rooted in male anatomy. Maybe, or maybe not. Who is to say that males are, clearly speaking, aggressive? Their muscular endowments are affirmed early on, and this manifests itself in the yearning of being the first at everything: food, sex, wealth, academic achievement, etc.? This observable behavior could be explained biologically. Freud, for example, observed and clinically documented the existence of a sex drive in humans that bleeds over other proclivities, of which being first in line is an example. Freud also wrote about Thanatos, the death instinct, of which the killer instinct is a part.

At the kindergarten stage, a rigid possibility of being male, being first, begins to assert itself as a construction of self-identity. At this stage, children begin to develop an interest in self-definition, while at the same time they learn to respect rules such as no kissing and that boys should play with boys and girls with girls. To some kids these rules do not make sense, and they challenge them at the expense of alienating themselves from their teachers. Others simply obey thoughtlessly and become willing conformists. Many conform reluctantly and hide resentments. It is these children in particular who are challenging authority and exploring new sew sexual identities. These children are the ones who silently suffer because they are developing an interest in boys like them and sometimes in girls, as well. They are, however, subtly and not so subtly reprimanded for feeling as they do. There are also disturbing cases of explicit bullying that takes place at many schools. It is notable that the suppression of possibilities is being subtly and brutally arrested at this foundational level of the developing of identities via the imaginations of young minds expressing themselves, openly declaring what they feel, and seeking to live their lives. In some cases, both teachers and parents are not sufficiently supportive of the children, and the consequence is profound unhappiness, at a crucial time of self-exploration. They are not even being given a chance to explore what they think they are, which they might be, and what they think they are not, which they might be. As impressive as it is, they are actually using their imaginary and intellectual capacities. We are not doing enough to encourage young minds in the making.[148] Instead, we kill their possibilities, by subjecting them to biological essentialism, and decide for them what we think they should be by pathologizing what they are exploring as possibilities and normalizing exactly what they are not feeling, by forcing them to conform to their essential natures, which we claim to know by the services of medical science and religious dogma. The power holders are systematically socializing reluctant children to be inauthentic, timid, and deeply afraid to be who they are. They are encouraged to stay inside the closet.

D. NORMS

Possibilities and Norms are inextricably intertwined. This is a time that is exemplary of how norms are constructed and become hegemonic, that is: dominant ideas that children think they must accept. Norms do obstruct possibilities, the otherwise free constructs of the imagination. When the imagination is allowed to do its work, it facilitates the project of the articulation and practice of freedom in the form of self-defining possibilities for the Self, as it comes in direct conflict with norms as the embodiments of established reality. Norms are to the established reality as possibilities are to freedom. These two languages of the Self affect one another intergenerationally.

Norms are nothing more than dominant ways of living, which many think are measures of normalcy written on stone that cannot be changed. Norms are processes of converting beliefs into normalities. Normalities are precisely outcomes of the norming process. Norms are transmitted by three agents: (1) the family, (2) education, and (3) the State. The example of the kindergarten children above will serve as an example again:

(1) The Family. Very early on children are socialized into believing that girls are supposed to play with girls and boys with boys. I hear and observe this at the school to which my son goes. Note immediately that children are being socialized to use sexual identities and situating themselves in gender norms, as if they are natural terms, such as water is a liquid. Children hear this from their teachers and classmates daily. The latter statement has been scientifically verified, and we are inclined to accept it as true. It establishes itself as a scientific

norm. Teachers repeat it and transmit it to their students as a scientific fact, which is also a norm, a description of normalcy. Parents learn it from teachers, churches, and their friends and reinforce it at home. On close scrutiny, this norm is merely a hypothesis according to the beliefs of some societies. Since there were ancient civilizations, (as I have argued in chapters 1–3), that did not have these beliefs, therefore those civilizations did not have the norms of gender. Families, however, are known to be the most primordial sites of the process on norming. Preschoolers and kindergarten children are the first victims of this norming process. Schools are the second sites of the norming process in a regressive and progressive sense, since there are regressive and progressive schools, as there are parents. The two sites of society mirror each other.

Regressively, parents subtly and sometimes aggressively tell their children that if they are boys, they can only be boys, and if they are girls, they can only be girls. Of course, some kids ask probing questions, and they are somehow shut off. The children get the message and shut up, and their feelings go deep in to the unconscious, and they begin to act out as they grow older. These are the types of children who transgress, and they are told that they need religious counseling and medical attention for the way they feel. The children are in this way trained not to construct values on their own but to repeat what they are told is the norm of the society, which they can't change. They must either adopt or perish.

Progressively, there are understanding parents who respect the feelings of their children and go with the flow. They listen to what is being said and encourage their children to be what they feel. They appreciate that their children are thinking, feeling, and choosing. Most importantly, they appreciate that their children trust them sufficiently to confide in them their inner lives. This is a win win situation, as it should be. They monitor at school, and other places, how their children are being treated by others, notably classmates, teachers, administrators, and all relevant others, so that their children are in a safe, supportive, and nurturing environment. They worry less about the sexual orientations that their children are exploring and are more mindful about their environment of exploration.

My humble opinion is that these are the parents who understand authentic parenting, an activity which is a composite of understanding, love, respect, and mindfulness. These are the necessary and sufficient conditions for raising children properly, as children are defining themselves by attending to their feelings and living out loud in the presence of progressive parents, who listen without judging, who observe attentively, and who encourage the process of exploration, without resorting to norms to obstruct the paths of self-invention.

(2) Education. Schools closely follow trends within the family, particularly when the State in power is regressive. Ideally, schools should be autono-

mous centers of perpetual exploration of imaginative possibilities, and safe environments where children of all ages can invent realities for themselves free of domination, intimidation, and fear. Progressive schools do that with enviable competence. Regressive schools do the opposite. Thus, schools are also major centers of legitimating some norms and delegitimizing others. They truly are homes of the norming process.

(3) The State. Like the family, the State also acts regressively and progressively. The behavior of the global state varies geographically. The State of the Global North is radically different from the state of the Global South. In both places, the binaries are treated with different philosophies. A state from the Global North, for example, passed legislation protecting the rights of individuals to practice a chosen sexual orientation. Such states must be applauded.

According to a survey, it is good news that progressive citizens are pushing the State to adapt to the changing attitudes regarding the binaries of man and woman. Transgender attitudes are taking a lead, slowly and surely.

The defense of the rights of those who are challenging the binaries are being legally protected by constitutional means, such as Title IX in the Global North, and attitudes are radically changing in the Global South. This is welcome news, but there is still more work to be done, particularly when citizens vote for a regressive State.

E. VALUES

Norms and values are so closely connected that I have to distinguish them very carefully, with razor sharp distinctions, which I will attempt below.

Norms are ways of life that are imposed on individuals by the family, the state, and schools, which insinuate themselves in the lives of individuals as if they are natural. There is very little room for asking questions about the norms themselves. Individuals are expected either to conform to these norms in order to live "normal lives," or suffer the consequences.

In contrast to norms, the quest for values itself is an inherent right of the thinking, imaginative, and reasonable individual, as is to ask existential questions, namely: how should I live and how do I construct a value that empowers me to live authentically, or, as the title of this book implies, how do I define myself? Values are attributes of the Self. Values, unlike norms, are predicated on thinking, as a gift for the Self, and by which the Self thinks deeply, imaginatively, and autonomously about how it should exist.

The Self is a value creating moral subject. Exploring possibilities of existence, as guided by the imagination, is a self-founded moral project of the Self that thinks, imagines, believes, and consciously constructs. The value foundation is the tangent where imagination, thought, and moral construction meet and propel desire to express its wants, aspirations, dreams, and passions. Whereas norms cement us to the existent values founded by others, who at one time chose for themselves, values give us that empowering right to figure out what's good and right for ourselves. Values, unlike norms, are not embedded in culture and tradition, although sometimes, they are subject to misuse. They wait for humans to uncover them, bring them out from hiding, and release them to emerge toward freedom.

I must now discuss certain values that humans want, and should want, in a safe and welcoming environment.

Sex and gender are nothing but values, anchored in a human anatomy. To that extent they are given parts of the human body. Of course, it is pointless to deny that we are biological beings. Biology is our material structure, on which we build the superstructure of values, such as our sex, and the gender that we can choose. The latter are possible values that we can mindfully develop, aware that our essence is biology, but that this essence in not our destiny. In fact there are no destinies, what there are are ways of life, styles of ethics and existence, that we consciously choose and then harness as thinking, imaginative, and spiritual beings.

Values are to the Self as norms are to society. Values empower us to creatively define what we want, where and how, particularly when we think freely. Norms, on the other hand, pressure us to either adjust or perish. Once we find values on our own, such as a given sexual orientation, it is hard to ask us to adjust to another sexual orientation, which has been normalized as a norm, and which we do not feel, or more importantly, wish to be. By this time, we have already defined ourselves; it is impossible to make us think otherwise. It is only those who have not dared to find values that authenticate them who easily succumb to norms, and when these norms conflict with how they feel, suppress their real feelings and live unhappy lives, inside closets, from which they never come out. In this melancholic state, they squander their lives and become resentful. Resentment is a condition produced by the inability to lead one's life on one's terms. It is the total absence of freedom and the right to map out one's course of living one's short life on earth.

It is in this particular sense that values become central to the life of the Self, particularly when there is an irreconcilable difference between authentic feelings and inauthentic norms. In such cases, those who are not living their lives are acting in "bad faith." This need not be a self-imposing imperative of the wrong kind. A good imperative would command the Self to live this short life authentically, by internally generated standards of excellence, in the quest of finding values that empower the Self by repeated practice. I call this yearning for self-found values the pragmatics of existence. The pragmatics of existence propels the Self to look for values that bring happiness, spiritual prosperity, and sharpness of mind. The sharpness of mind is honed by the repeated use of one's own reason, a reason that organizes the data that originates in the imagination and pushes forward the critique of norms and the flowering of original values. This is the task of reason.

F. REASON

Values are located by the imagination and thought through careful reasoning. Values originate in the imagination and are released by reason. Before we choose values, there are steps that we must follow intuitively and systematically. Intuition helps the imagination to find values, and reason immediately steps in to facilitate the findings of the imagination. Imagination and reason always work in concert to encourage the Self to make the right decisions. When we imagine how we would like to live, we first listen to the language of the heart, the seat of thinking, the place of authentic reasoning. We communicate with the heart by initiating a conversation solitarily. Solitude is a necessary and sufficient condition for founding any value, away from society's established reality mediated by norms. At this stage, imagination propels us to dream about ideal conditions anchored in values. Then reason joins the search and we initiate the second systematic effort of looking for values that truly make us happy and responsible to ourselves and those with whom we are destined to live. We discover what Lewis Gordon has called relationality, the idea that the Self exists only because other selves recognize it, and legitimate its existence.

This process of legitimation of the Self's existence empowers the Self to search deeply on its own and with the support of other selves who may be privately doing the same, because the Self is a value-creating being. When selves are so related, the search for values that empower and norms that disempower becomes the project of the reasoning and thinking Self. It is reason that trains the Self to distinguish values from norms, by realizing that norms, as the language of established reality, disempower the Self by making it dependent on the beliefs of others, whereas values, under ideal conditions, cultivate autonomous humans who use their values as sources of their identity. When individuals are bombarded by the daily news about the normalized binaries of race, sex, and gender, it is reason that empowers them to filter the dogmatized data and distinguish truth from falsity, such as the falsities of race, sex, and gender.

Distinguishing values that empower and norms that disempower is itself the outcome of reasoning, the reasoning of the thinking Self, which is the Self that thinks about what it is doing, as opposed to simply doing,—by adjusting to norms when norms function as principles that we cannot question, but rather, simply adjust to. Blind or uncritical adjustment is a serious flaw. The reasoning Self, which is aware of the flaw, can correct it by using its reasoning power. Using reason requires constant practice, or else reason falters in doing its job, which is empowering the Self to stand on its own feet.

Once a sexual orientation is felt deeply and chosen as a style of life, the chosen value must somehow be justified first and foremost to oneself, and when needed and expected, the individual must provide a reasoned response. This justification is not an imperative, however, as in certain situations the individual should not hide her sexuality in the closet. She must courageously and honestly be who she is and tell the world why she is so. This is particularly important in the context of the classroom, where sexual orientation might be the topic under discussion. In that case, the individual must be willing and capable of educating her classmates about what it means to be gay, particularly in a society that stigmatizes that sexual orientation. Hiding in the closet, although safe in unsafe places, is not a good practice in a safe environment. In such environments what is needed and useful is not hiding but coming out and patiently educating heterosexuals and others about the challenges of being gay, and proudly declaring it in the public and giving compelling reasons why the individual chose this particular lifestyle. Hiding is neither necessary nor useful for the growth of the Self. Hiding privatizes the rights of the individual in hiding and the rights of the public to know who that person is. The hiding does damage to the one who is hiding, by making that person live in bad faith. This attribute does not do good to anyone. Instead, it serves as a bad model for those who would like to come out but are told that it is dangerous to do so. I realize that not all situations are safe for this authenticity, but when certain environments provide the opportunity, the individual should positively exploit it, and be herself. Reason demands this imperative, and all self-defining individuals should respond to this calling, to this tender invitation for the sake of living an authentic life, with dignity.

G. FAITH

Reason could also work with faith. Faith is a necessary and sufficient condition for the complete power of reason to enable the Self to live authentically. Faith as a transcendental power is infinitely superior to reason, when reason stands alone. When reason joins faith, however, the outcome for the Self is sublime.

Faith is also a reasonable way of justifying values, including sexual orientations. Although most religions do not encourage certain sexual orientations, and the believer is caught in the middle of respecting the religious norms and her own feelings, reasoned faith demands that the individual chooses what she feels is right for her. Reason and faith could work in tandem to allow individuals to choose the appropriate styles of existence for them. Here, what the individual ought to do is first imagine a way of life, and an aesthetic, and ethics of existence. Second, the individual ought to think deeply and carefully about the imagined values, and third, if either religious or spiritual, develop a personal relationship with a given transcendent, and either meditate with or pray to this transcendent to help her live her life.

The suggestion that a religious person who is being jostled by the commitment to church and to her personal dreams takes us directly to addressing the issues of the Self as a desiring, moral, and actional subject, which is the theme of the conclusion, Self-Definition.

NOTES

146. Immanuel Kant, *Critique of Judgment* (Oxford, UK: Oxford Universtiy Press, 2007). The role of the imagination in the production of space and time, as the conditions of any experience is deeply analyzed by Kant in his *Third Critique of Judgement*, in *Art and Its Significance,* cited above. I follow Kant closely on his view of the Imagination. Here I assume Kant's view, but unlike him, I am specifically targeting the nature of the binaries and suggesting that Imagination can enable us to go beyond these fixed binaries to the uncharted water of possibilities.

147. Stephen David Ross (ed), *Art and Its Significance* (New York: New York State University Press, 1984). Herbert Marcuse has also suggested that our sexual lives are considerably larger and deeper that the way that Capitalism has confined them as commodities. *Eros and Civilization* and The *Aesthetic Dimension* are devoted to the exploration of the power of the Imagination and the possibilities which it defreezes from the Established Reality.

148. Kimberly A. Stieglitz, "Development, Risk, and Resilience of Transgender Youth," *Journal of the Association of Nurses in AIDS CARE.* 21, no. 3 (May–June 2010), 192–206.

Conclusion
Self-Definition

I will address themes in three parts:

A. The Desiring Subject
B. The Moral Subject
C. The Actional Subject

A. THE DESIRING SUBJECT

Long before the Self realizes that it is a moral and actional subject, as Plato was the first to acknowledge, (which then later became a Freudian project), the Self is a desiring subject. The Self is always desiring, consciously and unconsciously.

Consciously, we learned from Plato that the soul has three inseparable aspects: desire, spiritedness, and reason, and he recommends that desire and spirit be guided by reason if the Self is to live a peaceful life. The key is peace in the form of harmony, which the Self must seek, according to Plato's values, which are not necessarily the Self's values. Of course, Plato hopes that the global Self will desire Plato's values. Sadly, the global Self does not do so, voluntarily, but could be trained by philosophical education, which I will attempt below.

Unconsciously, the Self has three homes. There is the Id, that part of our mental life that recognizes no boundaries but desires everything: sex, food, shelter, and clothing, at any time, without limit. Then there is the Ego, which also desires but with self-imposed limitations. Finally, there is the Superego, symbolized by the authority of parents and tradition, which imposes further limits both on the Id and the Ego, (this too according to Freud).

Both Plato and Freud after him are right that the Self is primarily a desiring being, and this is not always a flaw, particularly when the Self is aware of its flaws and is willing and capable of addressing them. Desires are precisely what give the individual her uniqueness, a gift by which she can define a destiny for herself. This is particularly true when the desire empowers the individual to affect her destiny, and also when the said individual can thereafter regulate her desires in a manner she sees fit. Impressive is the outcome when desire can also submit itself to guidance by self-regulated reason in tandem with faith, in the important struggle of cultivating oneself by choosing a sexual orientation and a gender, freely and responsibly. Self-regulation of desire is the pivotal point of defining one's possibilities by monitoring the excesses of desire, which sometimes requires, as Plato thought, to expect those who have mastered themselves to guide those who have not, and cannot. As is well known, women and slaves were both thought to be incapable of self-regulation, thus necessitating that philosopher kings managed the affairs of those who could not manage their own lives.

Plato is right that unregulated desire can force the Self to experience avoidable outcomes when desire falls victim to the pressures of the Id, as Freud brilliantly discovered. That is only one of the orientations of desire. There are others that Plato and Freud discounted, namely, the possibility that the same Self that Plato and Freud feared is capable of regulating the whims of desire by employing imagination, reason, and faith responsibly. That desire is not always irrational. Often it may be, but not always.

Without desire the articulation of self-defining possibilities becomes impossible. One must desire a sexual orientation before one becomes that orientation. One must feel that he is a man before identifying himself as one. One cannot feel one way and be another. She must feel that she is a woman before she becomes a woman. She cannot be a woman when she feels that she is a man. Feeling is the highest and most authentic expression of desire. Where desire dwells, so does feeling, and feeling is so because desire says that it must be.

The desiring Self is therefore an expressive Self, a Self that is not afraid to declare her identity in broad daylight, in front of Heidegger's *they*. The desiring-self listens to the Id and the Ego, courageously follows the paths of the Id, specifically, the sexual paths that many people would like to follow, were it not for the aggressive presence of the Superego: parents, friends, churches and workplace colleagues—each passing a judgment and constricting freedom for the desiring subject, or the subject of desire.

B. THE MORAL SUBJECT

The desiring subject is also a moral subject. It is precisely morality that guides the Self to make correct choices as a subject of desire. The moral subject of our modern age, like all moral subjects of the past, is also critically aware, and when it is not, should be critically aware that the desires with which we are born can lead us astray unless we are willing to impose limiting conditions on the whims of our desires, when we must, and when we can. Just because we can desire infinitely, it does not follow that we should; it should in fact follow that precisely because our desires defy limitation, we must impose limitations on them. This imposition is an imperative that we must obey, if necessary, reluctantly. This awareness is what makes us distinctly human. Our attribute is not only thinking, although that is important, but on top of that, moral thinking, a form of thinking that empowers us to control our behavior, when our behavior most needs it.

As desiring beings, we are inclined to want to explore the possibilities of being human, of living our lives originally. That inclination comes naturally to us. Given our anatomy, we are inclined also to live a sexual orientation that nature assigns to us. Although we have only become men or women, and we may not have chosen these markers, we do not question them explicitly. We may not be living what we really feel, but we somehow manage to adjust to the inherited identities, with suppressed unhappiness, which we do not dare to voice at certain places and at certain times and within certain environments. We adjust as much as we can, and when we cannot, we practice what we feel hidden and away from people's gazes. It is at this point that we struggle with ourselves as moral subjects with desire, or as desiring moral subjects. When we think morally, we are really struggling with ourselves first, particularly when we live in bad faith.

Consider the following example. Individual A is secretly yearning that he becomes a woman, since his adopted sexual orientation is that he is a man and he plays the role of a male. His apparent Self is therefore that of a male. He is aggressive, dates women, and loves sports. He does all that males are supposed to do "perfectly," whatever that means. If one observes keenly, though, one notices that Individual A does not seem to be happy. He is trying to come out and declare his real Self, the Self that he feels, as opposed to the Self that he has adopted. There are complications on the way. He is aware that the environment in which he finds himself is not comfortable. The conversations he hears about sexual orientation are disconcerting. He has tried to come out to his colleagues at work but felt very uncomfortable, so he discontinued it. He tried to tell a woman about his condition. Again, there was no support. He took evening classes to check out the crowd there. No change, the same indifference prevailed. So, what can he to do but suffer silently and do the things he has decided to do in hiding? This behavior induces inauthenticity, living life without morality. He is being forced to lie. Moral subjects like Individual A live their lives in bad faith, against their wills. If it was up to him, Individual A would like to live authentically, in the open, and be who he is, proudly and normally gay. His situated existence precludes that possibility of self-definition, of being himself no matter what the consequences are. The pragmatics of existence forced him to live in hiding by wearing the mask of falsehood.

I recall a particular situation which I experienced in a class that I teach, where something similar happened. This is about Individual B.

He is young, barely twenty-two, intelligent, well spoken, and handsome. He recently came out to his roommate of four years, to whom he told that he is bisexual. His roommate, who was also his best friend, freaked out when he learned that Individual B is bisexual. He began making his best friend uncomfortable, so uncomfortable that he is looking for another place to live. When he told this story to his classmates, contrary to my expectations, he was received with indifference, and mild hostility. Nobody opened his mouth to comfort him. Silence was the response.

I was embarrassed for the classmates, whom I thought would at least say something. Of course, I do not know what the silence meant. It may be that the silence itself is the empathy—although I felt otherwise; but I am willing to hold judgement. I will leave the judgement to you, the reader.

Stories such as this run in the millions. They are not written about, until after the media decides to report on sensational stories. This is a story that will not make it to the media. It is a story of private pain, and the victims are too shy to share stories such as this.

Stories like this should be told. These are stories of anguish and despair, of people such as Individual B who have attempted to be heard and seen, while few hear or see them. These victims suffer silently. The world is not willing to hear them, unless they do something extraordinary, such as committing suicide, where upon the media will attend to them. That world where the ordinary is as important as the extraordinary can be changed only when the desiring and moral subjects choose to be actional beings, hence, the importance of analyzing actionality as the medium of self-definition in the next section.

C. THE ACTIONAL SUBJECT

The actional desiring and moral subject must act in order to be seen and heard, otherwise, she will be invisible to the bitter end, and by then death catches up with life, and the invisible desires of the moral subject are relegated to oblivion. This condition of invisibility can be changed by revolutionary political action in concert with classroom education, neighborhood, and workplace activities aiming at changing the established reality and the capitalist institutions that capitalize on the silence of the masses who suffer quietly.

The silence of all those who suffer because they cannot choose to be what they feel must. Silence must be replaced by revolutionary action.

Effectively organized social movements must become the agents of change, once the spark for change is lighted in the classroom by progressive teachers.

We must also give to the world when we can, thankfully. Giving to the world is itself a form of what I call actional thinking. Actional thinking is thanking, and thanking is a form of thinking, in the following sense:

> Spot Pond and its stirring beauty massage my soul. I see straight through the luster of the transparent blue water. I turn my steely eyes to the left, and there I see two white ducklings looking up, perfectly poised, and focused on the blue morning sky. I restlessly turn my tired neck to the left, and long lines of birds swimming away in perfect movement greet me. I said to myself this is for the eyes, the windows of the soul.
>
> I closed my eyes, looked up to the firmament, and thanked the creator of this universe, which is always there, firmly anchored on the foundations laid forever, by the creator, who does not have to account itself for the creation of the air, the water, the fire, and all these beings, of which the unthankful human is only one of a kind.
>
> I looked up again, and prayed to be put in a prayerful attitude, in the month of thanksgiving. As nearly as I can remember, I have yearned to get nearer to the voice of the transcendent, the voice of the generous lawgiver, waiting to be summoned to an environing by the prayerful and thankful attitude. I have known for years that to think is to thank, to pray is to think, to give is to think, and to receive is to thank. Only now, in my years of maturity am I slowly learning how to think by thanking and how to thank by thinking.
>
> In vain did I pray to get near the transcendent so as to really learn how to think—so difficult is learning how to think. Only when I genuinely thank do I sometimes experience the joy and pain of thinking. Then I feel fulfilled.
>
> To thank is to think, and to think is to thank. These simple and enigmatic words prominently trap me during the month of thanksgiving. How horrible I feel, when I cannot give anything, because I have nothing to give by way of material things, particularly money. But then that is not the only thing that I can give. There other non-things that I can give to a needy world, once I release myself from the hold of money, that dirty commodity, that turns the world aflame. Release from commodities is what I pray for, so that I can open myself to other possibilities, to different tasks. Generously giving money to my fellow sisters and brothers drenched in drinks, sorrow and hopelessness, propelled by the thanking attitude which gives immense pleasure, particularly when I do it with the correct moral attitude, which is the language of thanking by thinking, giving because I must, receiving because I am lucky.

It is exceedingly difficult to release myself from excessive self-love and love of family. The world is also my home, towards which I must be released. Surely love must begin with oneself, followed by the family, and ending with the world, but not necessarily in that order. The order ought to be open. I know that does not come easily to anybody, least of all me, the one who is pontificating now. When we are environed by the thankful attitude, we need not strictly follow the customary order of Self, family and the world. We can begin with that task that is the most imperative, the one that haunts our conscience, and commands our immediate moral attention. What matters is not where we begin but where we land, where we feel at home when we think through thanking.

I must learn how to perform my moral tasks joyfully and naturally in this thanksgiving month. Suffused by thankfulness I delve deeply into the caves of my soul and think about what I must do for the world. The concrete world is a world of pain, of sorrow, of hopelessness, of disease and poverty. Each of these facets of our marked days on this planet is gaping for my commitment. A child somewhere in the world had just died from AIDS; his mother had just killed herself upon the discovery of the brutal fact; wealth is being lavished on worthless things in the rich capitals of the world. A thankful disposition does not overlook these paradoxes. Their imposing presence on our conscience and consciousness creates sites of responsibility.

We cannot throw our hands and say too bad. The thankful horizon will refuse to release us from acts that display our want to transform the world through moral action.

Thanksgiving is the paradigmatic time to think by thanking and to thank by thinking. Now is the time to act. Now is the time to give. Now is the time to share. Now is the ultimate time to be human in a profound way. Take this valuable time to give, to share, and to receive.

Release yourself from Self and your duties will be disclosed to you through the invisible presence of the transcendent, the one who created you to use your moral intelligence and do things for the world.

Do not despair, thinking that your isolated moral action will not change the world. That is not the way of thinking by thanking. That is the way of not thinking because you are not thanking, but despairing. Despair, you must know, kills thinking.

[Originally published in Ethiomedia.com]

Bibliography

Abrams, Sil Lai. *Black Lotus: A Woman's Search for Racial Identity*. New York: Karen Hunter Publishing, 2016.

Adichie, Chimamanda Ngozi. *We Should All Be Feminists*. Nigeria: Fourth Estate, 2014

Afolayan, Adeshina, and Toyin Falola, eds. *The Palgrave Handbook of African Philosophy*. London: Palgrave MacMillan, 2017.

Alcoff, Linda Martín. *Visible Identities: Race, Gender, and the Self*. New York: Oxford University Press, 2005.

Alexander, Michelle. *The New Jim Crow: Mass Incarceration in the Age of Colorblindness*. New York: The New Press, 2010.

Ali, Suki. *Mixed-Race, Post-Race: Gender, New Ethnicities and Cultural Practices*. UK: Berg Publishing, 2003.

Andrews, Arin. *Some Assembly Required: The Not-So-Secret Life of a Transgender Teen*. New York: Simon & Schuster Books for Young Readers, 2015.

Angelou, Maya. *I Know Why the Caged Bird Sings*. New York: Ballantine Books, 2009.

Ariel, Levy. *Female Chauvinist Pigs: Women and the Rise of Raunch Culture*. New York: Free Press, 2005.

Aristotle. *Aristotle's Politics*. Oxford, UK: Clarendon Press, 1905.

Aronson, Amy. *The Gendered Society Reader*. Oxford, UK: Oxford University Press, 2000.

Baird, Forrest E., and Raeburne S. Heimbeck. *Asian Philosophy*. New York: Routledge, 2006.

Baldwin, James. *The Fire Next Time*. New York: Dial Press, 1963.

Baldwin, James. *Notes of a Native Son*. Boston, MA: Beacon Press, 1955.

Barrett, James. *Transsexual and Other Disorders of Gender Identity: A Practical Guide to Management*. Boca Raton: CRC Press, 2007.

Battles, Kathleen, and Wendy Hilton-Morrow. *Sexual Identities and the Media: An Introduction*. London: Routledge, 2015.

Baum, Bruce. *The Rise and Fall of the Caucasian Race: A Political History of Racial Identity*. New York: NYU Press, 2008.

Baumgardner, Jennifer. *Look Both Ways: Bisexual Politics.* New York: Farrar, Straus, and Giroux, 2007.

Bettie, Julie. *Women without Class: Girls, Race, and Identity.* Oakland: University of California Press, 2014.

Biegel, Stuart. *The Right to Be Out: Sexual Orientation and Gender Identity in America's Public Schools.* Minneapolis: University of Minnesota Press, 2010.

Bornstein, Kate. *Gender Outlaw: On Men, Women, and the Rest of Us.* New York: Vintage, 2016.

Brown, Claude. *Manchild in the Promised Land.* New York: Macmillan & Co, 1965.

Brown, Dee. *Bury My Heart at Wounded Knee: An Indian History of the American West.* New York: Holt, Rinehart & Winston, 1970.

Brownmiller, Susan. *Against Our Will: Men, Women and Rape.* New York: Simon & Schuster, 1975.

Burkett, Lori A., and Mark A. Yarhouse. *Sexual Identity: A Guide to Living in the Time Between the Times.* Lanham, MD: UPA, 2003.

Butler, Judith. *Gender Trouble: Feminism and the Subversion of Identity.* London: Routledge, 1990.

Butterfield, Rosaria. *Openness Unhindered: Further Thoughts of an Unlikely Convert on Sexual Identity and Union with Christ.* Pittsburgh, PA: Crown & Covenant Publications, 2015.

Cabral, Amilcar. *Return to the Source.* New York: Monthly Review Press, 1973.

Campbell, Joseph. *The Hero with a Thousand Faces.* New York: Pantheon Books, 1949.

Cecile Alduy, "The Philosopher, the Mother and the Baby," *Arcade: Literature, the Humanities & the World*, Stanford, CA: Stanford University, August 25, 2012.

Clark, Christine, and James O'Donnell, eds. *Becoming and Unbecoming White: Owning and Disowning a Racial Identity.* New York: Praeger, 1999.

Clark, Kenneth. *The Nude: A Study in Ideal Form.* London: Penguin Books, 1970.

Clark, Kenneth, ed. *Racial Identity in Context: The Legacy of Kenneth B. Clark.* Washington, DC: American Psychological Association, 2004.

Clausen, Jan. *Apples & Oranges: My Journey through Sexual Identity.* New York: Seven Stories Press, 2017.

Cleves, Rachel Hope. *Charity & Sylvia: A Same-Sex Marriage in Early America.* New York: Oxford University Press USA, 2014.

Coates, Ta-Nehisi. *Between the World and Me.* New York: Spiegel & Grau, 2015.

Cohler, Bertram, and Phillip L. Hammack. *The Story of Sexual Identity: Narrative Perspectives on the Gay and Lesbian Life Course.* New York: Oxford University Press, 2009.

Coles, Gregory. *Single, Gay, Christian: A Personal Journey of Faith and Sexual Identity.* Westmont, IL: IVP Books, 2017.

Colapinto, John. *As Nature Made Him: The Boy Who Was Raised as a Girl.* New York: Harper Perennial, 2006.

Collins, Patricia Hill. *Black Feminist Thought: Knowledge, Consciousness and the Politics of Empowerment.* London: Routledge, 2008.

Connell, Raewyn W. *Masculinities.* Cambridge: Polity Press, 1999.

Coolhart, Deborah and Rylan Jay Testa. *The Gender Quest Workbook: A Guide for Teens and Young Adults Exploring Gender Identity.* Oakland, CA: Instant Help, 2015.

Dallas, Joe. *Desires in Conflict: Hope for Men Who Struggle with Sexual Identity.* Eugene, OR: Harvest House Publishers, 2003.
Davis, Angela. *Angela Davis: An Autobiography.* New York: International Publishers, 2013
Davis, Angela. *Women, Race & Class.* New York: Vintage Books, 1981.
de Beauvoir, Simone. *The Second Sex.* New York: Vintage Books 1989, c1952.
Descartes, René. *Discourse on Method and Meditations.* New York: MacMillan, 1952.
Dhingra, Pawan. *Managing Multicultural Lives: Asian American Professionals and the Challenge of Multiple Identities.* Redwood City, CA: Stanford University Press, 2007.
Di Ceglie, Domenico, ed. *A Stranger in My Own Body: Atypical Gender Identity Development and Mental Health.* London: Routledge, 1998.
Dikötter, Frank. *The Construction of Racial Identities in China and Japan.* Hong Kong: Hong Kong University Press, 1997.
Douglass, Frederick. *Narrative of the Life of Frederick Douglass.* Boston, MA: Anti-Slavery Office, 1845.
Jane Dryden, "Hegel, Feminist Philosophy, and Disability: Rereading our History," *Disability Studies Quarterly* Vol 33, No 4 (2013).
Du Bois, W.E.B. (William Edward Burghardt). *The Souls of Black Folk; Essays and Sketches.* Chicago: A.G. McClurg, 1903.
Duffy, Brooke Erin. *(Not) Getting Paid to Do What You Love: Gender, Social Media, and Aspirational Work.* New Haven, CT: Yale University Press, 2017.
Dungy, Camille. *Guidebook to Relative Strangers: Journeys into Race, Motherhood, and History.* New York: W.W. Norton & Company, 2017.
Ehrensaft, Diane. *The Gender Creative Child: Pathways for Nurturing and Supporting Children Who Live Outside Gender Boxes.* New York: The Experiment, 2006.
Eisner, Shiri. *Bi: Notes for a Bisexual Revolution.* New York: Seal Press, 2013.
Equiano, Olaudah. *The Interesting Narrative of the Life of Olaudah Equiano, Or Gustavus Vassa, The African.* Scotts Valley, CA: CreateSpace Independent Publishing Platform, 2014.
Erickson-Schroth, Laura, ed. *Trans Bodies, Trans Selves: A Resource for the Transgender Community.* New York: Oxford University Press, 2014.
Esmail, Ashraf. *African American Identity: Racial and Cultural Dimensions of the Black Experience.* Lanham, MD: Lexington Books, 2014.
Fanon, Frantz. *A Dying Colonialism.* New York: Grove Press, 1965.
Fanon, Franz. *Black Skin, White Masks.* New York: Grove Press, 1967.
Fanon, Franz. *The Wretched of the Earth.* New York: Grove Press, 1963.
Fausto-Sterling, Anne. *Sexing the Body.* New York: Basic Books, 2000.
Feinberg, Leslie. *Trans Liberation: Beyond Pink or Blue.* Boston, MA: Beacon Press, 1999.
Fine, Cordelia. *Delusions of Gender: How Our Minds, Society, and Neurosexism Create Difference.* New York: W.W. Norton & Company, 2010.
Foucault, Michel. *The History of Sexuality: Volume 1: An Introduction.* New York: Vintage Books, 1980.
Foucault, Michel. *The Use of Pleasure: Volume Two.* New York: Vintage Books, 1985.
Friedan, Betty. *The Feminine Mystique.* New York: W. W. Norton & Company, 1963.

Fuller, Kay. *Gender, Identity, and Educational Leadership.* London: Bloomsbury Academic, 2015.
Funderburg, Lise. *Black, White, Other: Biracial Americans Talk About Race and Identity.* New York: Harper Perennial, 1995.
Garcia, Lorena. *Respect Yourself, Protect Yourself: Latina Girls and Sexual Identity.* New York: NYU Press, 2012.
Gaskell, Elizabeth. *The Life of Charlotte Brontë.* London: Smith, Elder & Co, 1857.
Gay, Roxanne. *Bad Feminist: Essays.* New York: Harper Perennial, 2014.
George, Sheldon. *Trauma and Race: A Lacanian Study of African American Racial Identity.* Waco, TX: Baylor University Press, 2016.
Giordano, Simona. *Children with Gender Identity Disorder: A Clinical, Ethical, and Legal Analysis.* London: Routledge, 2013.
Gordon, Lewis R. "Thoughts on two recent decades of studying race and racism," *Social Identities,* 2017, DOI: 10.1080/13504630.2017.1314924
Gordon, Gordon, *Is Philosophy Blue?* 15.
Gordon, Lewis. *Existentia Africana.* New York: Routledge, 2000.
Gordon, Lewis, *What Fanon Said.* New York: Fordham University Press, 2015.
Gordon, Lewis, "Black Existence in Philosophy of Culture," *Diogenes* 59, no. 3–4 (2014): 96–105. ICPHS 2013.
Gordon, Lewis, "Creolizing Critical Pedagogy and Political Theories of Education," *Review of Education, Pedagogy, and Cultural Studies* 40, no. 1(2017).
Greer, Germaine. The Female Eunuch. New York: Harper Perennial Modern Classics, 2008.
Gyekye, Kwame. *An Essay on African Philosophical Thought: The Akan Conceptual Scheme.* Cambridge, UK: Cambridge University Press, 1987.
Halberstam, Jack. *Female Masculinity.* Durham, NC: Duke University Press Books, 1998.
Halberstam, Jack. *In a Queer Time and Place: Transgender Bodies, Subcultural Lives.* New York: NYU Press, 2005.
Heidegger, Martin. *Being and Time,* trans. John McQuarrie and Edward Robinson. New York: Harper & Row, 1962.
Heidegger, Martin. *Discourse on Thinking.* New York: Harper & Row, 1966.
Heidegger, Martin. *What is Metaphysics?*
Heidegger, Martin. *What is Called Thinking?* New York: Harper Perennial, 1976.
Hellum, Anne, ed. *Human Rights, Sexual Orientation, and Gender Identity.* London: Routledge, 2016.
Helms, Janet E. *Black and White Racial Identity.* New York: Praeger, 1993.
Helms, Janet E. *A Race is a Nice Thing to Have.* United States: Microtraining Associates, 2007.
Hemmings, Clare. *Bisexual Spaces: A Geography of Sexuality and Gender.* London: Routledge, 2002.
Henry, Paget. *Caliban's Reason: Introducing Afro-Caribbean Philosophy.* London: Routledge, 2000.
Herzig, Rebecca M. *Plucked: A History of Hair Removal.* New York: New York University Press, 2015.

Hill, Katie Rain. *Rethinking Normal: A Memoir in Transition*. New York: Simon & Schuster Books for Young Readers, 2015.

Hoffman-Fox, Dara. *You and Your Gender Identity: A Guide to Discovery*. New York: Skyhorse Publishing, 2017.

hooks, bell. *Talking Back*. Boston, MA: South End Press, 1989.

Huntington, Samuel P. *The Clash of Civilizations and the Remaking of World Order*. New York: Simon & Schuster, 1997.

Ifekwunigwe, Jayne O, ed. *"Mixed Race" Studies: A Reader*. London: Routledge, 2004.

Incrocci, Luca and David L. Rowland, eds. *Handbook of Sexual and Gender Identity Disorders*. Hoboken, NJ: Wiley, 2008.

Izzard, Susannah. *Rethinking Gender and Therapy: Inner World, Outer World, and the Developing Identity of Women*. London: Open University Press, 2001.

James, William. *The Varieties of Religious Experience: A Study in Human Nature*. New York: Longmans, Green & Co., 1902.

Kant, Immanuel. *Critique of Judgment*. Oxford, UK: Oxford University Press, 2007.

Kant, Emmanuel. *Foundations of the Metaphysics of Morals*. New York: Prentice Hall, 1997.

Kant, Immanuel, and Norman Kemp Smith. *Immanuel Kant's Critique of Pure Reason*. Boston: Bedford, 1929.

Khanna, Nikki. *Biracial in America: Forming and Performing Racial Identity*. Lanham, MD: Lexington Books, 2013.

Kierkegaard, Soren. *A Kierkegaard Anthology*, ed. Robert Bretall. New York: Modern Library, 1936.

King Jr., Martin Luther. *Why We Can't Wait*. London: Signet, 2000.

Kinsey, Alfred. *Sexual Behavior in the Human Female*. Philadelphia: Saunders, 1953.

Kinsey, Alfred. *Sexual Behavior in the Human Male*. Philadelphia: Saunders, 1948.

Kiros, Teodros. *Zara Yacob: On the Rationality of the Human Heart*. Trenton, NJ: Africa World Press, 2002.

Kiros, Teodros, *Zara Yacob: Rationality of the Human Heart*, Trenton, NJ: Red Sea Press, 2005.

Kreiger, Irwin. *Helping Your Transgender Teen: A Guide for Parents*. Ashford, CT: Genderwise Press, 2011

Kuklin, Susan. *Beyond Magenta: Transgender Teens Speak Out*. Somerville, MA: Candlewick Press, 2014.

LaSalle, Mick. *Complicated Women: Sex and Power in Pre-Code Hollywood*. New York: St. Martin's Griffin, 2000.

LeFebvre, Michael. *The Gospel and Sexual Orientation*. Pittsburg: Crown & Covenant Publications, 2012.

Levithan, David. *The Full Spectrum: A New Generation of Writing About Gay, Lesbian, Bisexual, Transgender, Questioning, and Other Identities*. New York: Ember, 2006.

Madsen, Axel. *The Sewing Circle: Hollywood's Greatest Secret: Female Stars Who Loved Other Women*. London: Robson Books, 1995.

Mah, Adeline Yen. *Falling Leaves*. New York: Broadway Books, 1999.

McBride, James. *The Color of Water: A Black Man's Tribute to His White Mother*. New York: Penguin Group, 1996.

McWhorter, Diane. *Carry Me Home: Birmingham, Alabama: The Climactic Battle of the Civil Rights Revolution.* New York: Simon & Schuster, 2002.

Mead, Margaret. *Coming of Age in Samoa: A Psychological Study of Primitive Youth for Western Civilization.* New York: William Morrow Paperbacks, 2001.

Meyer, Elizabeth J., and Annie Pullen Sansfaçon, eds. *Supporting Transgender and Gender Creative Youth: Schools, Families, and Communities in Action.* Switzerland: Peter Lang, 2014.

Mock, Janet. *Redefining Realness: My Path to Womanhood, Identity, Love & So Much More.* New York: Atria Books, 2014.

Moran, Caitlin. *How to Be a Woman.* London: Ebury Press, 2011.

Morris, Desmond. *The Naked Ape: A Zoologist's Study of the Human Animal.* London: Delta, 1999.

Murphy-Shigematsu, Stephen L.H. *When Half Is Whole: Multiethnic Asian American Identities.* Redwood City, CA: Stanford University Press, 2012.

Muscio, Inga. *Cunt: A Declaration of Independence.* New York: Seal Press, 1998.

Nagoshi, Craig T., Julie L. Nagoshi, and Stephan/ie Brzuzy. *Gender and Sexual Identity: Transcending Feminist and Queer Theory.* New York: Springer, 2013.

Nelson, Maggie. *The Argonauts.* Minneapolis, MN: Greywolf Press, 2016.

Nkrumah, Kwame. *Consciencism.* New York: Monthly Review Press, 1964.

Obama, Barack. *Dreams from My Father: A Story of Race and Inheritance.* New York: Times Books, 1995.

Obenga, Théophile. *Ancient Egypt and Black Africa.* Trenton: Red Sea Press, 1996.

Obenga, Théophile. "Egypt: Ancient History of African Philosophy," in *A Companion to African Philosophy*, ed. Kwasi Wiredu. New York: Blackwell Publishing, 2004.

Ochs, Robyn and Sarah E. Rowly, eds. *Getting Bi: Voices of Bisexuals Around the World.* Boston, MA: Bisexual Resource Center, 2005.

Paris, Jennell Williams. *The End of Sexual Identity: Why Sex Is Too Important to Define Who We Are.* Westmont, IL: IVP Books, 2011.

Parker, Morgan. *There Are More Beautiful Things Than Beyoncé.* Brooklyn, NY: Tin House Books 2017.

Paulk, Anne. *Restoring Sexual Identity: Hope for Women Who Struggle with Same-Sex Attraction.* Eugene, OR: Harvest House Publishers, 2003.

Petrikowski, Nikki Peter, ed. *Gender Identity.* Berkeley Heights, NJ: Enslow Publishing Inc, 2016.

Phillips, Angela, ed. *Our Bodies, Ourselves.* New York: Touchstone, 2011.

Plato, *Plato's Phaedo.* Oxford, UK: Clarendon Press, 1911.

Rabaka, Reiland. *Concepts of Cabralism.* Lanham, MD: Lexington Books, 2014.

Rees, Emma L.E. *The Vagina: A Literary and Cultural History.* London: Bloomsbury Academic, 2013.

Rekers, George Alan. *Shaping Your Child's Sexual Identity.* Grand Rapids, MI: Baker Book House, 1982.

Rench, Janice E. *Understanding Sexual Identity: A Book for Gay and Lesbian Teens and Their Friends.* Minneapolis, MN: Lerner Publishing Group, 1992.

Ross, Stephen David (ed). *Art and Its Significance.* New York: New York State University Press, 1984.

Said, Edward W. *Orientalism.* New York: Pantheon Books, 1978.
Sax, Leonard. *Girls on the Edge: The Four Factors Driving the New Crisis for Girls—Sexual Identity, the Cyberbubble, Obsessions, Environmental Toxins.* New York: Basic Books, 2011.
Scholinski, Daphne. *The Last Time I Wore A Dress.* London: Riverhead Bks, 1997.
Shilts, Randy. *And the Band Played On: Politics, People, and the AIDS Epidemic.* New York: St. Martin's Press, 1987.
Skloot, Rebecca. *The Immortal Life of Henrietta Lacks.* New York: Crown, 2010.
Slater, Dashka. *The 57 Bus: A True Story of Two Teenagers and the Crime That Changed Their Lives.* New York: Farrar, Straus, and Giroux, 2017.
Solnit, Rebecca. *Men Explain Things To Me.* Chicago: Haymarket Books, 2004
Stein, Gertrude. *The Autobiography of Alice B. Toklas.* New York: Harcourt, Brace and Company, 1933.
Stieglitz, Kimberly A., "Development, Risk, and Resilience of Transgender Youth," *Journal of the Association of Nurses in AIDS CARE.* 21:3 (May–June 2010), 192–206.
Stryker, Susan. *Transgender History.* New York: Seal Press, 2008.
Tando, Darlene. *The Conscious Parent's Guide to Gender Identity: A Mindful Approach to Embracing Your Child's Authentic Self.* Avon, MA: Adams Media Corp, 2016.
Tatum, Beverly Daniel. *Why Are All the Black Kids Sitting Together in the Cafeteria: And Other Conversations About Race.* New York: Basic Books, 1997.
Taylor, Jared. *White Identity: Racial Consciousness in the 21st Century.* United States: New Century Books, 2011.
Te Velde, H. Seth, *God of Confusion: A Study of His Role in Egyptian Mythology and Religion.* Leiden: E.J. Brill, 1967.
Valenti, Jessica. *Full Frontal Feminism: A Young Woman's Guide to Why Feminism Matters.* New York: Seal Press, 2007.
Valenti, Jessica. *He's a Stud, She's a Slut, and 49 Other Double Stands Every Woman Should Know.* New York: Seal Press, 2008.
Valenti, Jessica. *The Purity Myth: How America's Obsession with Virginity Is Hurting Young Women.* New York: Seal Press, 2009.
Wade, Peter. *Blackness and Race Mixture: The Dynamics of Racial Identity in Colombia.* Baltimore, MD: Johns Hopkins University Press, 1993.
Washington, Booker T. *Up from Slavery: An Autobiography.* New York: Doubleday, Page, 1901
Washington, Harriet A. *Medical Apartheid: The Dark History of Medical Experimentation on Black Americans from Colonial Times to the Present.* New York: Doubleday, 2007.
Watkins, Gloria Jean. *Ain't I a Woman?: Black women and feminism.* Boston, MA: South End Press, 1981
Watkins, Gloria Jean. *Black Looks: Race and Representation.* London: Routledge, 2014
Watkins, Gloria Jean. *Feminism Is For Everybody: Passionate Politics.* Boston, MA: South End Press, 2000.
Watkins, Gloria Jean. *Killing Rage: Ending Racism.* London: Penguin, 1996.
Weisenfeld, Judith. *New World A-Coming: Black Religion and Racial Identity during the Great Migration.* New York: NYU Press, 2017.
West, Cornell. *Race Matters.* New York: Vintage Books, 1993.

Wijeyesinghe, Charmaine, ed. *New Perspectives on Racial Identity Development: A Theoretical and Practical Anthology.* New York: NYU Press, 2001.

Wijeyesinghe, Charmaine, ed. *New Perspectives on Racial Identity Development: Integrating Emerging Frameworks, Second Edition.* New York: NYU Press, 2012.

Wilkerson, Isabel. *The Warmth of Other Suns: The Epic Story of America's Great Migration.* New York: Random House, 2010.

Williams-Forson, Psyche A. *Building Houses Out of Chicken Legs: Black Women, Food, and Power.* Chapel Hill: University of North Carolina Press, 2006.

Wolf, Naomi. *The Beauty Myth: How Images of Beauty Are Used against Women.* London: Vintage, 1991.

Wollstonecraft, Mary. *A Vindication of the Rights of Woman.* New York: W.W. Norton & Company, 1988.

Woodward, Kath. *Questioning Identity: Gender, Class, Nation.* London: Open University Psychology Press, 2000.

Woodward, C. Vann. *The Strange Career of Jim Crow.* Oxford, UK Oxford University Press, 2001.

Woolf, Virginia. *A Room of One's Own.* London: Penguin Books, 1945.

Wright, Richard. *Black Boy.* New York: Harper & Brothers, 1945.

X, Malcolm, and Alex Haley. *The Autobiography of Malcolm X.* New York: Grove Press, 1965.

Yarhouse, Mark A. *Understanding Gender Dysphoria: Navigating Transgender Issues in a Changing Culture.* Westmont, IL: IVP Academic, 2015.

Yarhouse, Mark A. *Understanding Sexual Identity: A Resource for Youth Ministry.* New York City: Zondervan, 2013.

Yoshino, Kenji. *Covering: The Hidden Assault on Our Civil Rights.* New York: Random House, 2006.

Zucker, Kenneth, and Susan Bradley. *Gender Identity Disorder and Psychosexual Problems in Children and Adolescents.* New York: Guilford Press, 1995.

Index

actionality: for black self, 67; of decolonization, 68–69; of feminism, 87–88
actional subject, 112–14
African ontology: ego in, affirmation of, 85; examination of existence in, 84–86; okra in, 83–84, 85; origin of, 81; religion in relation to, 81–82; sumsum in, 83–85; Supreme Being role in, 82–84
African self: black self discovering, 68; culture for mobilizing, 72–74; nationalism in relation to, 69–70; personality of, 71–72; socialist path of autonomy for, 74–75
Alduy, Cecile, 41
anatomy: colonialism, of dying, 69; Hegel on, 44–45; imagination for defining, 98–99
Aphrodite, 32
Aristotle: on gender roles, 35–36; on imitation, 95; Plato in relation to, 31
Arjuna, 14–15
attachment: sex and gender as forms of, 13; struggle against worldly, 12
Atum Ra: creation of, 5, 8; gender and sexual identity of, 6, 8; as transcendentalist, 7

Aurobindo, Sri, 17–18
autonomy, 74–75

"bad faith," 78–79
Bad Faith and Anti Black Racism (Gordon), 76
beauty: Socrates on, 33–34; women as embodiment of, 46
becoming, 7
Being: as becoming, 7; forms of, 93; ontology as study of, 81
Being and Time (Heidegger), 51
The Bhagavad Gita, 14–15
black existence: "bad faith" and, 78–79; Euromodernity impact on, 80; freedom and home relationship regarding, 79–80; meaning of, 77; racism impacting, 76–78
black self: African self discovered by, 68; alienation of, 65–66; diagnosis of, 67; without ontology, 66–67. *See also* African self
Black Skin, White Masks (Fanon): on black self alienation, 65–66; *The Wretched of the Earth* connection to, 67
black women, 86–88
The Book of The Dead, 5
Brahman: as gender/sex neutral, 13–14, 92–93; *Upanishads* role of, 11

Buddhism, 29–30
Butler, Judith: on feminism, 61–62, 63; Foucault support from, 62–63

Cabral, Amilcar: on culture for African self, 72–74; for radical humanity, 75–76; on socialist path of autonomy, 74–75
capitalism: radical humanity from dissolution of, 76; sex and, 107n147
children: imagination of, 99–101; norms impacting, 101–3
Chinese thought, 21–27
Chuang Tzu: on dreams, 23–24; on knowledge, 25–26; on the Way, 26–27
colonialism: African personality for overthrowing, 71–72; black self impacted by, 66; culture for resisting, 73–74; decolonization relationship with, 68–69
Common Love, 32
Confucius, 21–22
Consciencism (Nkrumah): on African self, 71–72; history of philosophy examined in, 70–71
construction of values, 94–98
Critique of Judgment (Kant), 107n146
culture, 72–74

Dasein: death as destiny of, 53; manifestations of, 52–53; Meditative Thinking and, 54; as race, sex, and gender neutral, 51
de Beauvoir, Simone: on gender roles, 54–56, 57; on homosexuality, 57; on independent women, 58–59; on motherhood, 57–58; on sex and violence relationship, 54–55; on tools of power, 55–56; on women in love, 58
decolonization: mobilization for, 73–74; violence of, 68–69
Descartes, René: on gender equality, 40–41; meditations of, 41–42

desiring subject: as moral subject, 110–12; the Self as, 109–10
despair, 47, 114
destiny: in African ontology, 84; anatomy as, 98; death as, 53; desire for defining, 110
Discourse on Thinking (Heidegger), 53–54
divinity: of beauty, 33–34; of human body, 17–18; of women in ancient Egypt, 9
dreams: Chuang Tzu on, 23–24; of independent woman, 58–59
Dryden, Jane, 44

education, 102–3
ego: crisis of, 84–85; desire in relation to, 109–10; spirituality for overcoming, 83
Egypt, ancient: creation of gods in, 5–6, 8; gender complexity rooted in, 8; gender equality in, 8–9; Nun of, 5, 6–8, 11, 22–23, 92; ontology origin in, 81; Plato drawing from, 33; the Self in, 5–9, 92
Eightfold Path, 29
Electra complex, 55
enlightenment: characteristics of, 29; Suchness as realization of, 30
Enlightenment project: Descartes of, 40–42; Yacob of, 39–40
Euromodernity, 80
Existentia Africana (Gordon), 76, 77

faith: bad, 78–79; Buddhism on, 29–30; for self-definition, 106–7
family, 101–2
Fanon, Frantz: in Algeria, 69, 88n108; black condition diagnosed by, 67; on characterization of blacks and whites, 65–66; on decolonization, 68–69; for humanism, 70; for radical humanity, 75–76; as revolutionary violence theorist, 69–70
feminism: Butler on, 61–62, 63; of hooks, 86–88

Foucault, Michel: Butler support for, 62–63; on gender and sexual identity, 59–61
Foundations of the Metaphysics of Morals (Kant), 42
freedom, 79–80

gender and sexual identity: of ancient Egyptian gods, 5–6, 8; Butler on, 61–63; de Beauvoir on, 54–59; dreams in relation to, 24; Foucault on, 59–61; Heidegger on, 51–54; imagination influencing, 98–99; *The Republic* addressing, 34–35; *The Symposium* addressing, 31–34
gender equality: in ancient Egypt, 8–9; Descartes on, 40–41; Kierkegaard on, 46–47; Quran dismissal of, 37–38; Yacob on, 39–40
gender roles: Aristotle on, 35–36; Confucius on, 21–22; de Beauvoir on, 54–56, 57
gender/sex neutral: Atum Ra as, 8; Brahman as, 13–14, 92–93; Dasein as, 51; the Imperishable as, 13; Nun as, 5, 6, 92; the Self as, 92
Gender Trouble (Butler), 61
Gordon, Lewis: on "bad faith," 78–79; on Euromodernity, 80; on freedom and home relationship, 79–80; on meaning of blackness, 76; on racism, 76–78
Greek thought: Foucault on, 60–61; the Self in, 31–36, 93–94

the heart, 14
Heavenly Love, 32
Hegel, G. W. F.: on anatomy, 44–45; *The Phenomenology of Mind* by, 45–46
Heidegger, Martin: *Being and Time* by, 51; on death, 52–53; *Discourse on Thinking* by, 53–54
Henry, Paget: African religions focus of, 81–82; on existence in African ontology, 84–86; on Supreme Being in African ontology, 82–84
heterosexuality, 62
The History of Sexuality (Foucault), 59–60
home: freedom relationship with, 79–80; of the Self, 109–10
homosexuality: de Beauvoir on, 57; as disease, 60; Foucault on, 60–61; *The Symposium* on, 32
hooks, bell, 86–88
human body: as illusion of senses, 41; perfection of, 17–18
humanism, 70

imagination: Kant on, 107n146; possibilities from, 99–101; for self-definition, 98–99
imitation, 95–96
immortality: love as quest for, 33; price of, 11–12; of the Soul, 14–15
imperialism: African personality for overthrowing, 71–72; Confucius for Chinese, 22; culture for resisting, 73–74; radical humanity from dissolution of, 76
the Imperishable: Aurobindo on, 17–18; *The Bhagavad Gita* on, 14–15; *Upanishads on*, 13
inborn nature, 22
independent woman, 58–59
Indian thought: from *The Bhagavad Gita*, 14–15; from *Upanishads*, 11–13, 14, 17–18
Isis hymn, 9
Isness: of Nun, 5; of Tao, 22–23

Kant, Immanuel: on imagination, 107n146; morality contradiction of, 43–44; on moral worthy action, 42–43
Kierkegaard, Soren, 46–47
King Jr., Martin Luther, 97
knowledge, 25–26
Krishna, 14–15

Lao Tzu, 22–23
love: Common and Heavenly, 32; Kierkegaard on, 46–47; as quest for immortality, 33; sex replacing, 59; *The Symposium* views on, 31–34; women in, 58

meditation: of Descartes, 41–42; Suchness attained through, 29–30; *Upanishads* on, 12–13
Meditative Thinking, 54
men: Aristotle on role of, 35–36; Confucius on role of, 21–22; Quran on, 37–38; women defined by, 55
modeling, 96–98
modernity: Euromodernity, 80; gender and sexual identity and, 51–63; Yacob as founder of, 39–40
moral subject, 110–12
moral worthy action, 42–43
motherhood, 57–58

narcissist woman, 58
nationalism, 69–70
Nkrumah, Kwame: on African self, 71–72; history of philosophy examined by, 70–71; for radical humanity, 75–76
norms: reasoning for distinguishing values from, 105–6; of self-definition, 101–3; values in relation to, 103–5
Nun: Brahman in relation to, 11; characteristics of, 5, 7–8; Obenga on, 6–7; as race, sex, and gender neutral, 5, 6, 92; Tao in relation to, 22–23

Obenga, Theophile: on gender equality in ancient Egypt, 8–9; on Nun, 6–7
okra, 83–84, 85
oppression pillars, 87

Pausanias, 32
perfection of the body, 17–18
Phaedo (Plato), 93–94
Phaedrus, 31–32

The Phenomenology of Mind (Hegel), 45–46
pillars of oppression, 87
Plato: Aristotle in relation to, 31; on desire, 110; on imitation, 95; on the Self, 31–35, 93–94; on Soul aspects, 109
possibilities: norms impacting, 101–3; the Self as composite of, 91–92; of self-definition, 99–101

Quran, 37–38

race neutral: Dasein as, 51; Nun as, 5, 6, 92; Quran as, 38; the Self as, 92
racism: black existence impacted by, 76–78; hooks on, 86
radical humanity, 75–76
reasoning: faith in relation to, 106–7; for self-definition, 105–6
relationality: "bad faith" attack on, 78–79; Egyptian origin of, 5
religion: African ontology in relation to, 81–82; sexual orientation influenced by, 106–7
The Republic (Plato), 34–35
research summary, 1–2

the Self: as actional subject, 112–14; in ancient Egypt, 5–9, 92; Aristotle on, 35–36; becoming as distinguishing attribute of, 7; Buddhism on, 29–30; Chuang Tzu on, 23–27; as composite of possibilities, 91–92; Confucius on, 21–22; Descartes on, 40–42; as desiring subject, 109–10; Hegel on, 44–46; in Indian thought, 11–15; Kant on, 42–44; Kierkegaard on, 46–47; Lao Tzu on, 22–23; as moral subject, 110–12; Plato on, 31–35, 93–94; as race, sex, and gender neutral, 92; self-construction and, 1; senses imposing limitations on, 25; Yacob on, 39–40
self-construction: Aurobindo on, 18; forms of, 94–95; imitation for,

95–96; modeling for, 96–98; the Self and, 1
self-definition: absolutes and, 24–25; faith for, 106–7; imagination for, 98–99; imitation and, 95–96; the Imperishable present in all, 13; meaning of, 1, 91; modeling and, 96–98; norms of, 101–3; Nun as exercise in, 5; possibilities of, 99–101; quest for recognition as, 45; reasoning for, 105–6; self-construction for, 94–98; values impacting, 103–5
Self-realization, 17–18
senses: human body as illusion of, 41; the Self limitations from, 25
sex: capitalism and, 107n147; Foucault on, 59–60; as violence, 54–55
sexual orientation: Confucius on, 22; difficulty with, 111–12; faith and, 106–7; heterosexuality, 62; homosexuality, 32, 57, 60–61; imagination for discovering, 98–99; imitation of, 95–96; modeling of, 96–97; nondiscrimination of, 40; norms impacting, 101–3; possibilities of, 99–101; reasoning for justifying, 105–6; as Self expression, 91; values influencing, 103–5. *See also* gender and sexual identity
socialism, 71–72, 74–75
Socrates, 32–34
the Soul: immortality of, 14–15; as the Imperishable, 13; Plato on aspects of, 109; *The Republic* examination of, 34–35
The State, 103
Suchness, 29–30
sumsum, 83–85
Superego, 109, 110
Supermind, 18
Supreme Being, 82–84
The Symposium (Plato), 31–34

Tao, 22–23
thankfulness, 113–14
thinking thing concept, 41–42
transcendentalist, 7

unenlightenment, 29
ungendered and unsexed identity. *See* gender/sex neutral
Upanishads: Aurobindo in disagreement with, 17–18; *The Bhagavad Gita* in relation to, 14; Brahman role in, 11; on the Imperishable, 13; on meditation, 12–13; on quest for immortality, 11–12
The Use of Pleasure (Foucault), 60–61

values: construction of, 94–98; reasoning for distinguishing between norms and, 105–6; self-definition impacted by, 103–5
violence: of decolonization, 68–69; revolutionary, 69–70; sex as, 54–55; against women, 87–88

the Way, 26–27
women: Aristotle on role of, 35–36; black, 86–88; Butler on, 61–62; Confucius on exclusion of, 21–22; divinity of, in ancient Egypt, 9; as embodiment of beauty, 46; historical lenses on, 56; independent, 58–59; Kierkegaard on, 46–47; men defining, 55; myths about, 56–57; narcissist, 58; *The Phenomenology of Mind* on, 45–46; Quran on, 37–38; sex as violence toward, 54–55; violence against, 87–88
The Wretched of the Earth (Fanon): *Black Skin, White Masks* connection to, 67; on decolonization, 68–69

Yacob, Zara, 39–40

About the Author

Teodros Kiros is Professor of Philosophy and Literature at Berklee College of Music, a Non Resident Dubois Fellow at Harvard University, host and Producer of African Ascent and author of thirteen books, including two novels, *Hirut and Hailu and other Short Stories* and *Cambridge Days*, and an award-winning book *Self-Construction and The Formation of Human Values*.